Intermediate Classical Aramaic: Book II

ܐܝܬܝܩܘܢ ܕܠܫܢܐ ܐܪܡܝܐ ܥܬܝܩܐ ܬܪܝܢܐ

Aramaic Language Chaldean Dialect

ܐܪܡܝܐ ܠܫܢܐ ܟܠܕܝܐ ܠܗܓܐ

© 2021 by Michael J. Bazzi and Dr. Rocco A. Errico

Edited by Michael J. Bazzi, Dr. Rocco Errico, and Roy M. Gessford

ISBN: 978-1-941464-40-3

PCCN: Library of Congress Control Number: Pending

All Rights Reserved. Printed in the United States of America. No part of this book may be used or reproduced in any manner whatsoever without written permission except in the case of brief quotations embodied in critical articles and reviews.

PUBLISHED BY

Intermediate Classical Aramaic II is published by arrangement with the Noohra Foundation, Bazzi Publishing, and Let in the Light Publishing.

Cover photo credit: Bernadit Seman. The Walls of Babylon.

Let in the Light Publishing

www.letinthelightpublishing.com

Contents

Chapter	Page
1. BDOL Letters and Nouns	1
2. Personal Pronouns	10
3. Verbs: General Rules	22
4. Demonstrative and Interrogative Pronouns	30
5. Verbs: Usage	39
6. Verbs: Past Tense Indicative Mood (Perfect Tense)	52
7. Verbs: Present Tense Indicative Mood	64
8. Future Tense Indicative Mood (Imperfect Tense)	71
9. Verbs: The Imperative and Infinitive Moods	83
10. Dictionary	90

CHAPTER ONE
BDOL Letters and Nouns

Chapter 1
Reading

VOCABULARY

Wages, Payment	ܐܓܪܐ
Oh!	ܐܘ. ܐܘܗ
Resentment (anger that never forgives)	ܐܟܬܐ
Hosanna	ܐܘܫܥܢܐ
Shame	ܒܗܬܬܐ
He chose	ܓܒܐ
Gold	ܕܗܒܐ
Pure	ܕܟܝܐ
Is	ܗܘ ܐܝܬܘܗܝ
Mind	ܗܘܢܐ
Just, Righteous	ܙܕܝܩܐ
Justice, Righteousness	ܙܕܝܩܘܬܐ
Sight, Aspect, Example	ܚܙܬܐ
Seer	ܚܙܝܐ
Happiness, Good Fortune	ܛܘܒܐ
Judah	ܝܗܘܕܐ
He put on, he wore or has worn	ܠܒܫ

Faithful	ܡܗܝܡܢܐ
Death	ܡܘܬܐ
He spoke	ܡܠܠ
Lady-(title), Mistress	ܡܪܬܐ
My Lady	ܡܪܬܝ
Praiseworthy, Glorious	ܡܫܒܚܐ
Prophet	ܢܒܝܐ
Silver, Money	ܣܐܡܐ
Fool	ܣܟܠܐ
He ascended, went up, climbed	ܣܠܩ
Maker	ܥܒܘܕܐ
Strength, Force, Might	ܥܘܫܢܐ
Vigilant	ܥܝܪܐ
Labor	ܥܡܠܐ
Prudent, Smart, Bookmark	ܦܩܚܐ
Iron	ܦܪܙܠܐ
Saint, Saints	ܩܕܝܫܐ ܩܕܝܫܐ̈
Mercy – Only pl.	ܪ̈ܚܡܐ

Vigilance	ܥܺܕܽܘܬܳܐ
Boast	ܥܘܽܒܕܽܘܬܳܐ
Simon	ܫܶܡܥܽܘܢ
Tribe, Race, Generation	ܥܰܕܰܬܳܐ

Review: Book 1, p.73, Ch. 2 – rule 4, the four B D O L (Bdhol) letters. See also the Inseparable Particles (Prefixes - ܡܶܬܬܰܠܝܳܢܶܐ) pp 84-85. These four prefixes change the case of a noun in the sentences. There are six cases for a noun in Aramaic:

1. **NOMINATIVE** – the case of the subject : ܡܰܠܟܳܐ

   The king is good.   ܡܰܠܟܳܐ ܐܺܝܬܰܘܗܝ ܛܳܒܳܐ

2. **VOCATIVE** – The case used in a direct address: ܡܰܠܟܳܐ

   Oh King!.   ܐܽܘ ܡܰܠܟܳܐ

3. **GENITIVE** – The case of designation (used mostly of the possessor – of) : ܕܡܰܠܟܳܐ

   The brother of the king said, "I am good".   ܐܰܚܳܐ ܕܡܰܠܟܳܐ ܐܶܡܰܪ : ܐܶܢܳܐ ܐܢܳܐ ܛܳܒܳܐ

4. **DATIVE** – The case of the indirect object – to or for: ܠܡܰܠܟܬܳܐ

   The king gave the queen three horses.   ܡܰܠܟܳܐ ܝܰܗܒ ܠܡܰܠܟܬܳܐ ܬܠܳܬ ܣܽܘܣܘܳܢ

5. **ACCUSATIVE** – The case of the direct object of the verb: ܠܰܒܪܶܗ

   The King commanded his son.   ܡܰܠܟܳܐ ܦܩܰܕ ܠܰܒܪܶܗ.

6. **ABLATIVE** – The case of cause, agency, location and instrument – in, with, by, through, by means of, etc: ܒܒܰܝܬܳܐ

   The king was in the house.   ܡܰܠܟܳܐ ܐܺܝܬܰܘܗܝ ܗܘܳܐ ܒܒܰܝܬܳܐ.

RULES FOR THE ܠ ܘ ܕ ܬ LETTERS

1- When the letter Waw - ܘ - (and) is prefixed to a word, it serves as a co-coordinative conjunction: ܘܡܠܟܐ - w'malka, and the king.

2- The particles ܐܘ or ܐܘܿ are rarely placed before nouns to designate the vocative case. However, on occasions when the particles are used in a sentence, a lamadh (ܠ) is prefixed to the noun or to any adjective or pronoun employed substantively that follows the particles: ܐܘ ܠܟ ܟܗܢܐ - oh, Oh, you priest! ܐܘ ܠܡܠܟܐ ܕܓܒܟ - Oh, the king who chose you!

3- The lamadh (ܠ) of the accusative case may be dropped from a noun (not a pronoun), if the meaning is not ambiguous. It is generally retained when the direct object is complement to the objective suffix of the verb. (See C).

A) USAGE WITH LAMADH (ܠ)

Call on the Lord. ܩܪܐ ܠܡܪܝܐ   Honor your father!. ܝܩܪ ܠܐܒܘܟ

B) USAGE WITHOUT LAMADH (ܠ)

Receive Oh Lord, our service and our prayers!

ܩܒܠ ܡܪܢ ܬܫܡܫܬܢ ܘܨܠܘܬܢ.

C) WITH (ܠ) AS COMPLEMENT TO THE OBJECTIVE SUFFIX

Jesus destroyed death. ܝܫܘܥ ܒܛܠܗ ܠܡܘܬܐ.

He opened heaven. ܦܬܚܗ ܠܫܡܝܐ.

4- The prepositions ܒ and ܠ are also added to some particles, mainly, adverbs of time and place:

   a- Here - ܗܵܪܟܵܐ , over here - ܠܗܵܪܟܵܐ

   b- Where - ܐܲܝܟܵܐ , to where - ܠܐܲܝܟܵܐ

   c- When - ܐܸܡܲܬܝ , until when - ܠܐܸܡܲܬܝ

   d- Yesterday - ܐܸܬܡܵܠܝ , of yesterday - ܕܐܸܬܡܵܠܝ

5- The ܒܓܕܟܦܬ letters receive the zlama psheeqa ܸ instead of the usual pthaha ܲ when prefixed to words which dropped their initial ܐ . (See Ch. 2, p. 79, rule 13: B - ܫܬܐ , CLASSICAL ARAMAIC I)

   a- Six - ܫܬܐ for (ܐܫܬܐ), ܒܸܫܬܐ and ܠܸܫܬܐ

   b- Bond - ܐܣܵܪܐ , ܒܸܣܵܪܐ and ܕܸܣܵܪܐ

6- The letter ܕ is also used as a relative pronoun (that, which, who, whom, and whose) and it introduces a relative clause. Dalath prefixed to verbal forms and particles as a relative pronoun admits the case-forming preposition.
Examples: ܟܵܬܹܒ - he writes, ܕܟܵܬܹܒ - He who writes; ܠܕܟܵܬܹܒ - To him who writes.

7- When several nouns in the same case are connected by the coordinative conjunction
   ܘ Waw, the case –forming preposition prefixed to the first noun may or may not be prefixed to the subsequent nouns.

   Example: ܒܥܹܕܬܐ ܘܒܝܬܐ or ܒܥܹܕܬܐ ܘܒܒܝܬܐ

SYNTAX

The copula "is" or "are" may be omitted in Aramaic.

   Example: ܒܐܘܪܚܐ ܕܩܘܫܬܐ ܫܠܵܡܐ - In the path of truth is peace.

THE DAYS OF THE WEEK:

Sunday	ܚܕܒܫܒܐ
Monday	ܬܪܝܢܒܫܒܐ
Tuesday	ܬܠܬܒܫܒܐ
Wednesday	ܐܪܒܥܒܫܒܐ
Thursday	ܚܡܫܒܫܒܐ
Friday	ܥܪܘܒܬܐ
Saturday	ܫܒܬܐ

NOTE: The first five days, Sunday through Thursday, are the cardinal masculine numbers one through five, ܚܕ - ܚܡܫܐ, added to the word bshabba ܒܫܒܐ

EXERCISE

A- Translate the following sentences into Aramaic.

1- Hosanna to the son of David (ܕܘܝܕ)
　
_____

2- Glory to God in the highest!.
　
_____

3- The reward of justice is life.
　
_____

4- Oh, Lord God of heaven and earth!.
　
_____

5- The Holy Spirit spoke through the prophets and apostles the living word of God.
　
_____

6- The faithful (pl) and righteous are good and holy.
　
_____

7- John spoke the truth with a pure and prudent mind.
_____

8- The Father and the Son and the Holy Spirit are one.
_____

9- To the living and holy God.
_____

10- You were a good example to all (ܠܟܠܗܘܢ) the faithful in truth and with love and power with prayers of night and day.
_____

11- The saints on earth are the salt of the earth.
_____

12- The Lord of all put on power and strength.
_____

13- Oh, (ܐܘ) king of heaven and earth!
_____

14- The path of light is life and the path of darkness (ܚܫܘܟܐ) is death.
_____

B- Translate the following sentences into English.

ܐ. ܐܠܗܐ ܕܫܡܝܐ.

ܐ. _____

ܒ. ܩܕܝܫܐ ܕܥܠܡܐ.

ܒ. _____

ܓ. ܚܕ ܗܘ ܐܠܗܐ ܚܝܐ.

ܓ. _____

ܕ. ܬܫܒܘܚܬܐ ܒܡܪ̈ܘܡܐ.

ܕ. ____________________

ܗ. ܫܠܡ ܠܥܡܐ.

ܗ. ____________________

ܘ. ܘܐܡܗ ܕܐܠܗܐ ܕܡܫܝܚܐ.

ܘ. ____________________

ܙ. ܡܪܐ ܕܥܝܪ̈ܐ ܘܡܠܐܟ̈ܐ.

ܙ. ____________________

ܚ. ܐܠܗܐ ܕܟܠ: ܐܒܐ ܕܢܘܗܪ̈ܐ.

ܚ. ____________________

ܛ. ܢܫܒܚܘܢ ܫܡܐ ܕܡܠܟ̈ܐ.

ܛ. ____________________

ܝ. ܛܘܒܐ ܠܥܡܐ : ܛܘܒܐ ܠܥܠܡܐ.

ܝ. ____________________

ܝܐ. ܟܬܒܐ ܠܥܕܬܐ ܕܩܘܕܫܐ.

ܝܐ. ____________________

ܝܒ. ܐܝܠܢܐ ܕܦܪܙܠܐ ܦܘܡܐ ܕܕܒܐ ܐܠܦܐ ܕܫܡܝܐ :ܐܝܕܐ ܕܢܡܠܐ

ܝܒ. ____________________

ܝܓ. ܫܘܒܚܐ ܗܘܝ ܠܐܒܐ ܒܪܐ ܫܒܝܠܐ.

ܝܓ. ____________________

CHAPTER TWO
Personal Pronouns

Reading

ܐ. ܐܡܝܢ ܐܡܪ ܐܢܐ ܠܟ ܕܝܘܡܢܐ ܥܡܝ ܬܗܘܐ ܒܦܪܕܝܣܐ.

ܒ. ܘܐܡܪ ܠܐܡܗ: ܐܢܬܬܐ. ܗܐ ܒܪܟܝ. ܘܐܡܪ ܠܬܠܡܝܕܐ ܗܘ: ܗܐ ܐܡܟ.

ܓ. ܐܒܝ: ܒܐܝܕܝܟ ܣܐܡ ܐܢܐ ܪܘܚܝ.

ܕ. ܦܢܝܐ ܬܫܥܐ ܒܫܥܬܐ ܩܥܐ. ܘܐܡܪ: ܐܝܠ ܐܝܠ ܠܡܢܐ ܫܒܩܬܢܝ.

ܗ. ܘܠܗ ܗܒܝܠ ܬܠܡܝܕܘܗܝ ܟܠܗܘܢ ܫܡܝܐ.

ܘ. ܐܢܐ ܐܢܐ ܠܚܡܐ ܕܚܝܐ. ܐܢܐ ܐܢܐ ܢܘܗܪܗ ܕܥܠܡܐ.

ܙ. ܐܢܐ ܐܢܐ ܬܪܥܐ. ܐܢܐ ܐܢܐ ܪܥܝܐ ܛܒܐ.

ܚ. ܐܢܐ ܐܢܐ ܢܘܚܡܐ ܘܚܝܐ. ܐܢܐ ܐܢܐ ܐܘܪܚܐ ܘܫܪܪܐ ܘܚܝܐ.

ܛ. ܐܢܐ ܐܢܐ ܓܦܬܐ ܕܫܪܪܐ. ܘܐܒܝ ܗܘ ܦܠܚܐ.

ܝ. ܒܪܫܝܬ ܐܝܬܘܗܝ ܗܘܐ ܡܠܬܐ. ܘܗܘ ܡܠܬܐ ܐܝܬܘܗܝ ܗܘܐ ܠܘܬ ܐܠܗܐ ܘܐܠܗܐ ܐܝܬܘܗܝ ܗܘܐ ܡܠܬܐ.

VOCABULARY

As, like (adj.)	ܐܝܟ
He says	ܐܡܪ
Doctor, Physician	ܐܣܝܐ
Oven, Furnace	ܐܬܘܢܐ

Creator	ܒܳܪܽܘܝܳܐ
A brave or valiant man, Giant	ܓܰܢܒܳܪܳܐ
Vine	ܓܦܶܬܳܐ
Dawned, Shone	ܕܢܰܚ
Desert	ܕܰܒܪܳܐ
Arm	ܕܪܳܥܳܐ
Now, Then, Thus, So, Therefore, For	ܗܳܟܺܝܠ
Turned, Returned, Converted	ܗܦܰܟ
Victory	ܙܳܟܽܘܬܳܐ
Darkness	ܚܶܫܽܘܟܳܐ
Sinful (feminine)	ܚܰܛܳܝܬܳܐ
Was destroyed	ܚܪܶܒ
Destroyed, Devastated	ܚܪܳܒ
Land, Dry land	ܝܰܒܫܳܐ
Today, This day	ܝܰܘܡܳܢܳܐ
Canopy, Pavilion, Veil	ܝܳܪܺܝܥܬܳܐ
Inheritance	ܝܳܪܬܽܘܬܳܐ

Teaching, Learning, Doctrine	ܝܘܠܦܢܐ
Cherubim	ܟܪܘܒܐ
Vineyard	ܟܪܡܐ
Herald, Messenger, Preacher	ܟܪܘܙܐ
Resurrection, Recovery, Revival	ܢܘܚܡܐ
Put, Place	ܣܝܡ ܣܘܡ ܣܡ
Peoples, Nations	ܥܡܡܬܐ
Husbandman, Laborer, Vinedresser	ܦܠܚܐ
Paradise, Park, Garden (Persian)	ܦܪܕܝܣܐ
He cried out, called out	ܩܥܐ
Pastor, Shepherd, Bishop	ܪܥܝܐ
Beginning, Origin, First beginning	ܪܫܝܬܐ
Left, Departed, Forgave, Permitted, Kept	ܫܒܩ

NAMES OF THE MONTHS

April	Nisan	ܢܝܣܢ
May	Eeyar	ܐܝܪ
June	Hzeeran	ܚܙܝܪܢ

July	Tamuz	ܬܲܡܘܿܙ
August	Ab	ܐܵܒ
September	Eelul	ܐܝܼܠܘܿܠ
October	Tishreen I	ܬܸܫܪܝܼܢ: ܐ
November	Tishreen II	ܬܸܫܪܝܼܢ: ܒ
December	Kanon I	ܟܵܢܘܿܢ: ܐ
January	Kanon II	ܟܵܢܘܿܢ: ܒ
February	Shwat	ܫܒܵܛ
March	Adhar	ܐܵܕܵܪ

NOTE: The Aramaic months begin on the 14th of the English months.

REVIEW: Book 1, Chapter 5, p.118, Personal Pronouns.

Personal Pronouns are declined by prefixing ܕܝܼܠ The genitive preposition ܕ becomes ܕܝܼܠ. The first person singular takes Hwasa, ܻ with the prefixes ܕܝܼܠ.

DECLENSION OF THE PERSONAL PRONOUN

POSSESIVE PREPOSITION: ܕܝܼܠ

My - ܕܝܼܠܝܼ   Our - ܕܝܼܠܲܢ

Your (M S) - ܕܝܼܠܘܼܟ݂   Your (M PL) - ܕܝܼܠܵܘܟ݂ܘܿܢ

Your (F S) -	ܕܝܠܟܝ	Your (F PL) -	ܕܝܠܟܝܢ
His -	ܕܝܠܗ	Their (M PL) -	ܕܝܠܗܘܢ
Her -	ܕܝܠܗ	Their (F PL) -	ܕܝܠܗܝܢ

DATIVE AND ACCUSATIVE: (to).

To me -	ܠܝ	To us -	ܠܢ
To you (M S) -	ܠܟ	To you (M PL)	ܠܟܘܢ
To you (F S) -	ܠܟܝ	To you (F PL)	ܠܟܝܢ
To him -	ܠܗ	To them (M PL)	ܠܗܘܢ
To her -	ܠܗ	To them (F PL)	ܠܗܝܢ

ABLATIVE (in, with, by, etc)

In me -	ܒܝ	In us -	ܒܢ
In you (M S) -	ܒܟ	In you (M PL) -	ܒܟܘܢ
In you (F S) -	ܒܟܝ	In you (F PL) -	ܒܟܝܢ
In him -	ܒܗ	In them (M PL) -	ܒܗܘܢ
In her -	ܒܗ	In them (F PL) -	ܒܗܝܢ

General Notes

The ܗ of the third person singular, masculine and feminine, is silent whenever the ܗ has no vowel. Thus in ܕܝܠܗ and ܕܝܠܗ̇ the final hey ܗ is not pronounced. But the ܗ is pronounced whenever ܗܘ or ܗܝ is joined to the declined personal pronoun in the third person singular, masculine and feminine. Hence ܒܗܘܗܘ or ܒܗܘ is pronounced as behoo, ܠܗܘܗܘ or ܠܗܘ as lehoo, etc. Like the ܗ of the third person singular, masculine and feminine, when it is affixed to other words and carries no vowel, it remains silent. Example: ܟܠܒܗ - his dog, ܡܠܟܬܗ̇ preposition or verb, they are known as inseparable pronouns or pronominal suffixes – enclitic forms.

BASIC RULES FOR THE PERSONAL PRONOUN

1- There is an archaic form of the personal pronoun "we" - ܚܢܢ and it is - ܐܢܚܢܢ. This form is found only in ancient manuscripts.

2- The vowel ܀ on the initial Alap of ܐܢܐ does not have the full value of or power of a complete vowel. Hence the correct pronunciation of ܐܢܐ is " I'na " and " Inna ".

3- There are some late Aramaic grammarians who have interpreted the ܗܘ and ܗܝ and their plural as the third person pronouns. But ܗܘ and its other forms are compounds of ܗܐ - "behold" and the personal pronouns ܗܘ ܆ ܗܝ and their plural. Thus, ܗܘ is a combination of ܗܘ + ܗܐ meaning "behold him" ܗܝ is a combination of ܗܝ + ܗܐ meaning "behold her". However ܗܘ is never affixed to or inflected with other words.

4- The first person plural ܚܢܢ " we " is used instead of the singular "I" ܐܢܐ by kings and high dignitaries when speaking of themselves. Then again, in later centuries (from the 12th century C.E.) the second person plural "you" ܐܢܬܘܢ was employed in the place of the singular, " you " ܐܢܬ, when addressing respectable persons.

5- The personal pronouns are enclitically used in the place of the verb " to be " in the indicative present tense. The enclitic forms generally agree with the subject in gender, number and person together with the noun, pronoun, adjective or participle to which they may be joined. The third person enclitic forms are also used with the first and second personal pronouns as subjects, agreeing with them in gender and number.

EXAMPLES: You are the Christ. - ܐܢܬ ܗܘ ܡܫܝܚܐ ; (I am) I am he. - ܐܢܐ ܗܘ ; (You are) You are they. - ܐܢܬܘܢ ܐܢܘܢ etc.

6- In the enclitic form the Alap of ܐܢܐ and the ܗܘ, ܗܝ are always occulted.
EXAMPLES: I am - ܐܢܐ ܐܢܐ ; this is - ܗܢܐ ܗܘ ; I am nice. - ܐܢܐ ܫܦܝܪܐ . The enclitics ܗܘ and ܗܝ sometimes drop the ܗ .

EXAMPLES: ܡܢܘ - (ܡܢ ܗܘ) = Who is he?
And ܡܢܘ - (ܡܢܐ ܗܘ) = What is …. Etc.

7- The ܗ of ܗܘ and ܗܝ is changed to ܝ when they are repeated - ܗܘܝܘ from ܗܘ, ܗܘ, He is; the same; the very one is : ܗܝ from ܗܝ ܗܝ - The same is; she is; the very one is. In Aramaic such repetition has a sense of intensity. Ex. ܗܘܝܘ ܡܠܟܐ - The same is the king; it is king himself.

8- The enclitic ܗܘ occurs sometimes as a corroborative and sometimes as more ornament.
ܠܐܚܪܢܐ ܗܘ ܡܣܟܝܢܢ – we wait for another.

9- ܗܘ : ܗܝ Coming after a word terminating in ܳ lose their vowel. Ex. ܕܝܢܐ ܗܘ When ܗܝ is preceded by a word terminating in ܳ and having only two letters, of which the second is not duplicated, the final ܳ is changed to a ܰ . Ex. ܗܝ + ܡܢܐ = ܡܢܗܝ - What is? Etc.

17

10- The third person plural forms are: masculine - ܗܶܢܘܿܢ ; Feminine - ܗܶܢܶܝܢ . They are - ܐܶܢܘܿܢ, ܗܶܢܘܿܢ ; they are (f) - ܐܶܢܶܝܢ ܗܶܢܶܝܢ . These forms with alap as pronouns occur only:

   a) As a direct object to transitive verbs. Ex. ܩܶܛܠܶܬܗ ܐܶܢܘܿܢ – I killed him.

   b) For emphasis in the place of ܗܶܢܘܿܢ . Ex. ܐܶܬܬܩܶܠܘ ܐܶܢܘܿܢ ܒܟܺܐܦܐ. – They stumbled against a stone.

11- ܚ Of ܚܢܰܢ and ܬ of ܐܰܢ̄ܬܘܿܢ and ܐܰܢ̄ܬܶܝܢ are occulted when they follow participles and contracted forms of nouns and adjectives.

   Ex. ܟܳܬܒܺܝܢ ܚܢܰܢ – we are writing or we write. ܚܦܺܝܛܺܝܢ ܚܢܰܢ – we are diligent. ܐܰܠܳܗܶܐ ܐܰܢ̄ܬܘܿܢ – you are Gods! If ܚ and ܬ follow unconstructed forms of nouns and adjectives, they are not occulted.

   Ex. ܡܰܠܟܶܐ ܐܰܢ̄ܬܘܿܢ – You are kings. ܚܦܺܝܛܳܐ ܚܢܰܢ – We are diligent.

12- For the sake of intensity the third person pronoun, singular, is repeated and the particle ܟܰܕ is placed in the middle of the repeated pronoun.

   Ex. ܗܘܿ ܗܘܿ ܟܰܕ ܗܘܿ . ܗܝܿ ܟܰܕ ܗܝܿ : ܗܶܢܘܿܢ ܟܰܕ ܗܶܢܘܿܢ. - the same. ܕܺܝܠܶܗ ܟܰܕ ܕܺܝܠܶܗ Of the same. ܒܳܗ̇ ܟܰܕ ܒܳܗ̇. – with the same etc.

13- The personal pronoun as a subject is often omitted when it stands as a predicate and often becomes an enclitic after the most important word of the predicate. Ex. ܙܰܟܳܝ ܐ̱ܢܳܐ. – I am innocent, instead of ܐܶܢܳܐ ܙܰܟܳܝ. ܐܺܝܠܳܢܳܐ ܗ̱ܝ ܕܚܰܝ̈ܶܐ. - She is the tree of life, instead of ܗܝܿ ܐܺܝܠܳܢܳܐ ܕܚܰܝ̈ܶܐ. etc.

14- The personal pronoun as a subject is generally placed at the beginning of a sentence and then it is repeated enclitically to form the copula.

   Ex. ܐܶܢܳܐ ܥܰܦܪܳܐ ܐ̱ܢܳܐ ܘܩܶܛܡܳܐ – I am dust and ashes. ܐܶܢܳܐ ܐ̱ܢܳܐ ܡܳܪܝܳܐ – I am the Lord.

15- The predicate agrees with its subject in gender, number and person. It may either precede or follow the subject.

Ex. ܡܳܪܝܳܐ ܐܶܡܰܪ ܠܡܘܫܶܐ – The Lord said to Moses. ܝܶܫܘܿܥ ܕܶܝܢ ܐܶܡܰܪ ܠܶܗ - But Jesus told him.

16- A pronoun as the subject of a sentence is often omitted.

Ex. ܗܘ ܡܬܰܚ ܫܡܰܝܳܐ – He spread out the heavens. ܘܦܰܪܶܩ ܠܥܳܠܡܳܐ – He saved the world.

17- A pronoun as the subject of a sentence may be placed before the predicate, often, for a sense of emphasis.

Ex. ܐܶܢ ܨܳܒܶܐ ܐܰܢ̱ܬ – If only you are willing. ܘܶܐܢܳܐ ܡܚܰܘܶܐ – and I am to show it to you or and I shall show you.

Exercise

A – Translate the following sentences into Aramaic.

1- Praise to you, oh God! Praise to you, oh Creator! Glory to you, oh Christ the king!

2- You are the Christ, the son of the living God.

3- We are the people of God.

4- Prayer ascended from the sea and from the pit and from the furnace.

5- You are my light and my truth.

6- He chose life and not death, love and not power.

7- Therefore this generation turned to God and his teaching.

8- The light shone in the darkness and destroyed Joseph's canopy.

9- The cherubim and the preachers of truth were in paradise.

10- He said, "Today, I am the true vine of heaven."

B- Translate the following sentences into English.

ܐ. ܐܢܐ ܐܝܬܝ ܐܠܗܐ ܫܪܝܪܐ.

ܒ. ܐܢܬܘܢ ܐܝܬܝܟܘܢ ܓܒܪܐ ܕܕܗܒܐ.

ܓ. ܗܘܝܢ ܡܠܦܢܐ ܐܠܗܝܐ.

ܕ. ܗܘܝܢ ܩܪܒ ܠܥܠ ܡܕܒܚܐ.

ܗ. ܐܢܐ ܐܝܬܝ ܡܠܟܗܘܢ ܘܡܪܐ ܕܪܩܝܥܐ ܕܫܡܝܐ.

ه. ܩܪܳܐ ܝܶܫܘܿܥ ܠܬܰܠܡܺܝ̈ܕܰܘܗ̱ܝ.

و. ܪܳܡܐ ܕܣܰܘܓܳܐ ܝܶܫܘܿܥ ܠܶܗ ܚܰܝ̈ܠܶܐ ܘܬܶܕܡܪ̈ܳܬܳܐ.

ح. ܩܪܳܐ ܡܳܪܰܢ ܐܳܬܶܐ ܢܶܒܗܺܝ ܥܰܠܡܳܐ ܚܰܕܬܳܐ ܘܐܰܬܪܳܐ

ط. ܐܳܬܶܐ ܢܶܒܗܺܝ ܗܳܘܶܐ ܕܥܳܠܡܳܐ.

ي. ܗܘܺܝ ܒܰܪ ܕܬܶܕܡܪ̈ܳܬܳܐ.

Chapter Three
Verbs: General Rules

Reading

VOCABULARY

Luke	ܠܘܩܐ
Forever	ܠܢܠܡ
On account of	ܡܛܠ
Humility	ܡܟܝܟܘܬܐ
Reproof, Rebuke, Reprimand	ܡܟܣܢܘܬܐ
Destroys, Obliterate	ܡܘܒܕ
Part, Portion	ܡܢܬܐ
Protector	ܢܛܘܪܐ
Hope, Assurance	ܣܒܪܐ
Enemy, One who hates	ܣܢܐܐ
Party, Feast, Festival	ܥܕܥܕܐ
It was or became obscure	ܥܛܝ
Fled, Ran away	ܥܪܩ
Prevailed, Became strong	ܥܫܢ
Strong, mighty	ܥܫܝܢܐ
Met	ܦܓܥ
Salvation	ܦܘܪܩܢܐ

Became insipid, tasteless	ܦܟܗ
Divided	ܦܠܓ
Flew	ܦܪܚ
Pharaoh	ܦܪܥܘܢ
Approached	ܩܪܒ
Rode	ܪܟܒ
Pardon, Forgiveness	ܫܘܒܩܢܐ
Rule over	ܫܠܛ
Was pleased	ܫܦܪ
True	ܫܪܝܪܐ
Truly	ܫܪܝܪܐܝܬ
In truth, truly	ܒܫܪܪܐ
Trust, Confidence	ܬܘܟܠܢܐ
Repentance	ܬܝܒܘܬܐ
Honest, Upright, Straight	ܬܪܝܨܐ

REVIEW: Book 1, The Verb, The Defective verbs and Unit Two, Past Tense Indicative Mood (Prefect Tense).

25

General Notes

1- The third person masculine singular (3 M. S.) perfect tense, indicative mood is the primary form or stem of a verb. A soft taw - ܬ, is suffixed to the verb for the feminine gender as given in the following examples of the trilateral strong verbs, known as the P'al ܦܥܠ strong verbs. These verb will have a Pthaha ܰ or a zlama psheeqa ܶ on the second radical, the first and the third radicals remaining non-vocalized in the primary form.

2- Suffixing the feminine ending - ܬ to the 3rd F. S., the first radical receives the zlama psheeqa ܶ the second radical loses its vowel; and the third radical receives pthaha ܰ and becomes hard. This change of vowels and aspirations takes place in all P'al ܦܥܠ verbs except concave and lamad weak verbs.

Examples:

Masculine		Feminine	
He wrote -	ܟܬܒ	She wrote -	ܟܶܬܒܰܬ
He saved -	ܦܪܩ	She saved -	ܦܶܪܩܰܬ
He did, He made-	ܥܒܕ	She did or she made -	ܥܶܒܕܰܬ
(S) Was or became dark -	ܚܫܟ	(f) Was or became dark -	ܚܶܫܟܰܬ

3- There are two endings each for the third person masculine and feminine plural in the indicative perfect: Masculine - ܘܢ:ܘ ; Feminine – ܝܢ or it is written exactly like the 3rd m. s. as in ܟܬܒ . The plural forms most commonly used are:

Masculine ܟܬܒܘ and Feminine ܟܬܒ Examples

Masculine		Feminine	
They wrote -	ܟܬܒܘ	They wrote -	ܟܬܒ
They wrote -	ܟܬܒܘܢ	They wrote –	ܟܬܒܝܢ
They fell -	ܢܦܠܘ	They fell -	ܢܦܠ

26

They fell - ܢܦܠܘܢ   They fell - ܢܦܠܝܢ

4- For the perfect indicative second person (M.& F.; S. & PL.) and for the first person plural the enclitic form of the respective personal pronouns are affixed to the primary form (i.e. 3 M.S.) There are two endings for the first person plural; for the first only one noon - ܢ is affixed to the primary form as in ܢ and for the second two - as in ܟܬܒܢ .

5- When the first person singular ending (which is a soft taw - ܬ) is affixed to the primary stem, the first radical receives a zlama psheeqa (̣) and the third radical receives a zlama qashya (̤) and become hard; the second radical loses its vowel just as in the 3rd f.s. (see note no. 3 with examples).

6- The first person perfect is of common gender; the second and third person have separate endings for masculine and feminine genders. In the perfect first person singular and in the 3rd f.s., the third radical becomes hard. In all other cases it is soft; the first radical is always hard and the second always soft.

EXAMPLES:

Common Gender – First Person

I wrote - ܟܬܒܬ   We wrote - ܟܬܒܢ or ܟܬܒܢܢ

Masculine   **Feminine**

You wrote (S) ܟܬܒܬ   You wrote (S) ܟܬܒܬܝ

You wrote (PL) ܟܬܒܬܘܢ   You wrote (PL) ܟܬܒܬܝܢ

EXERCISE

A- Translate the following sentences into Aramaic.

1- The truth pleased Luke.

2- My hope is in God my savior.

3- I am the tue light of the world and I am the true path of the nations. (Peoples).

4- He converted the sea into dry land.

5- His love became strong over us (ܥܠܝܢ).

6- God is the true rock.

7- He fell into the pit he has made.

8- He rode the black horse of death.

9- He flew over the temple of the great God of life and truth.

10- He saved them for the sake of his name (ܫܡܗ).

B- Translate the following sentences into English.

ܐ. ܢܦܠܘܢ ܗܘܘ ܩܕܡ ܠܒܥܠܕܒܒܐ.

ܒ. ܡܫܒܚܘܗܝ ܕܡܘܫܐ ܢܒܝܐ ܗܘܘ ܩܕܡ ܒܢܝܐ ܕܥܡܐ ܙܥܘܪܐ.

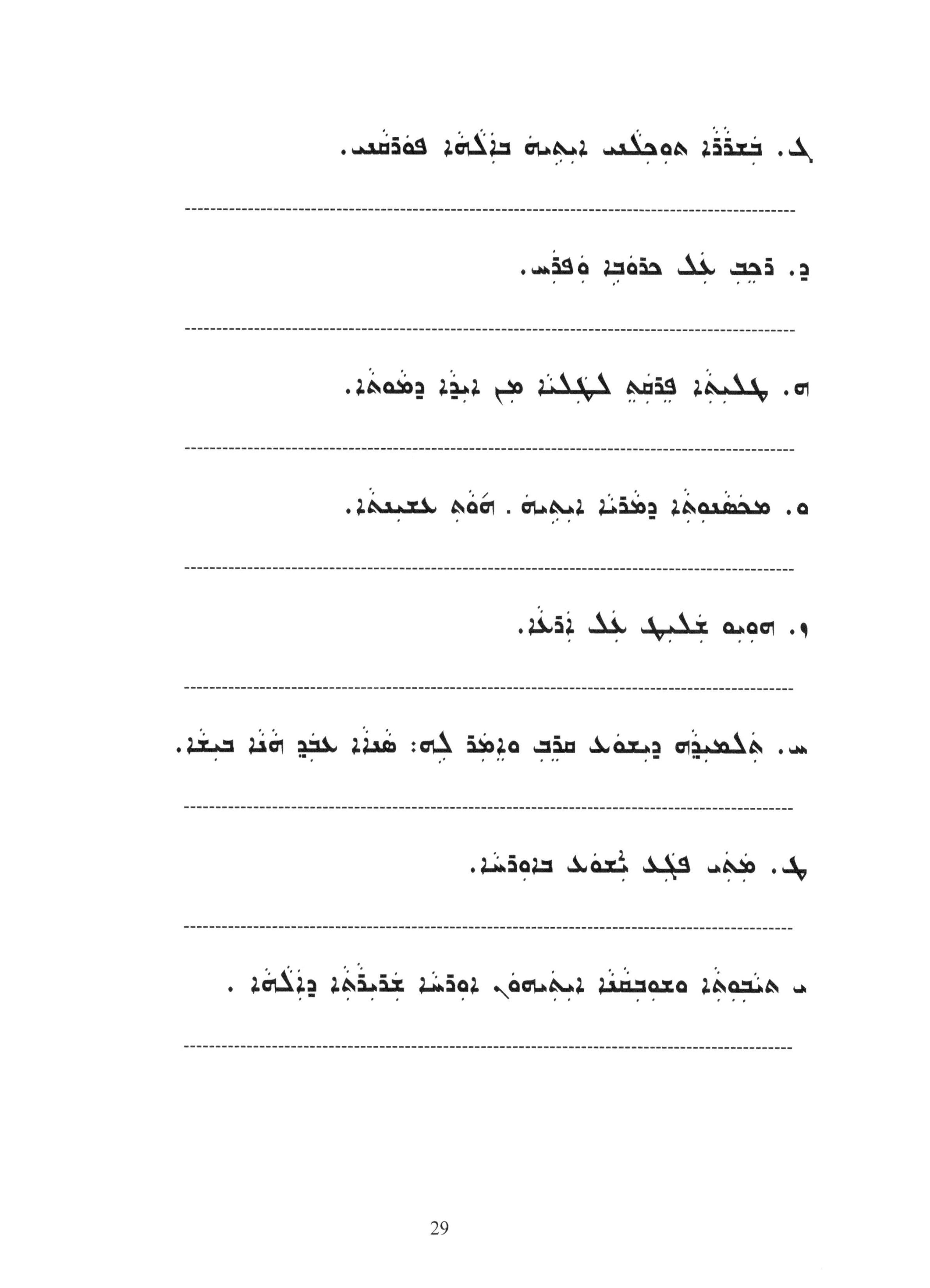

CHAPTER FOUR

DEMONSTRATIVE AND INTERROGATIVE PRONOUNS

DEMONSTRATIVE AND INTERROGATIVE PRONOUNS

Reading

ܐ. ܟܡܐ ܡܠܟܐ ܡܠܟܘ ܕܐܬܘܪ ܒܝܘܡܬܐ ܩܕܡܝܐ.

ܒ. ܗܢܐ ܛܘܪܐ ܪܡܐ ܐܝܬܘܗܝ ܛܘܪܐ ܩܕܝܫܐ.

ܓ. ܠܡܢܐ ܕܡܝܟ ܫܡܫܐ.

ܕ. ܦܐܪܐ ܕܐܝܠܢܐ ܐܝܬܘܗܝ ܛܒܐ.

ܗ. ܐܝܕܐ ܗܝ ܒܪܬܟ.

ܘ. ܝܘܡܐ ܠܡܢܐ ܒܒܝܬܐ ܕܡܕܝܢܬܐ ܐܠܗܐ ܠܟܠܗܘܢ ܥܠܡܝܢ.

ܙ. ܐܝܠܢܐ ܛܒܐ ܐܝܬܘܗܝ ܒܓܢܬܐ ܗܕܐ.

ܚ. ܒܪܫܝܬ ܒܪܐ ܐܠܗܐ ܫܡܝܐ ܘܐܪܥܐ.

ܛ. ܡܫܝܚܐ ܐܡܪ: ܐܝܢ. ܐܚܐ. ܐܢܐ ܐܝܬܝ ܐܠܗܐ.

ܝ. ܦܫܘܛ ܡܫܝܚܐ ܠܐܝܕܐ ܗܠܝܢ ܠܛܘܪܐ.

VOCABULARY

NOTE: The vocabulary is arranged alphabetically (Aramaic) and no longer according to parts of speech.

Tree	ܐܝܠܢܐ
Day (time)	ܐܝܡܡܐ
Yes	ܐܝܢ

Mother, Mothers	ܐܡܐ ܐܡܬܗܐ
Lamb	ܐܡܪܐ
Earth	ܐܪܥܐ
Created	ܒܪܐ ܒܪܝ
This (M)	ܗܢܐ
Time	ܘܕܢܐ
Saw	ܚܙܐ
Mountain	ܛܘܪܐ
Day (24 hrs.)	ܝܘܡܐ
Crowd	ܟܢܫܐ
Forever and ever	ܠܥܠܡ ܥܠܡܝܢ
Bread	ܠܚܡܐ
Night	ܠܝܠܝܐ
Spoke	ܡܠܠ
Word	ܡܠܬܐ
Let there be	ܢܗܘܐ
Fruit	ܦܐܪܐ

Beginning	ܬܕܥܒܝ
Door (Gate)	ܦܬܚܐ

Demonstrative Pronouns: ܣܠܟ ܥܡܕܬܐ ܡܫܢܝܬܐ

There are 11 demonstrative pronouns and they are divided into two classifications:

Near and Distant.

A- NEAR

Masculine Singular	-	This	ܐܗܐ
Feminine Singular	-	This	ܐܕܐ
M and F Plural	-	These	ܐܢܝ
Masculine Singular	-	That	ܗܘ
Feminine Singular	-	That	ܗܝ
Masculine Plural	-	Those	ܗܢܘܢ
Feminine Plural	-	Those	ܗܢܝܢ

B- DISTANT

Masculine Singular	-	That	ܗܘ
Feminine Singular	-	That	ܗܝ
Masculine Plural	-	Those	ܗܢܘܢ
Feminine Plural	-	Those	ܗܢܝܢ

Interrogative Pronouns: WHO and WHICH

Masculine Singular	ܐܝܢܐ
Feminine Singular	ܐܝܕܐ

Masculine & Feminine Plural   ܐܝܠܝܢ

All three above pronouns are used for persons and things. What, how - ܡܢܘ

ܡܢܐ ، ܡܢܕ are used for things regardless of gender or number.

How many - ܟܡܐ is used for people and things regardless of number and gender. The Aramaic word "How many" is a combination of the letter kap ܟ (much) and the word "how" - ܡܐ .

NOTE: Who is, What is (used for persons or things) may be contracted ܐܝܢܘ . This contraction is a combination of ܐܝܢܐ and ܗܘ .

The same contraction occurs with – who is it ܡܢܘ. This word is a combination of ܡܢ and ܗܘ .

The same rule applies for what is it ܡܢܘ . This word is a combination of ܡܢܐ and ܗܘ

A relative pronoun ܫܡܐ ܥܡܐ ܕܡܢ occurs when the interrogative is followed by a Dalath which precedes a verb.

Example: ܡܢ ܕܐܝܬ ܠܗ ܟܠܬܐ ܚܬܢܐ ܗܘ .   He who has a bride is a groom.

The Dalath ܕ before the verb ܐܝܬ ܠܗ represents a relative pronoun following the interrogative He who ܡܢ . This rule applies to all interrogative pronouns. A more detailed explanation is forthcoming in future chapters in the study of verbs.

Translate the following phrases into English and underscore the demonstrative pronoun in each sentence.

2. ܗܢܐ ܛܠܝܐ ܕܝܗܒܬ ܠܟܬܒܐ .

ܒ. ܗܕܐ ܛܠܝܬܐ ܐܝܬܝܗ ܟܫܝܪܬܐ.

ܓ. ܗܠܝܢ ܡܠܟ̈ܐ ܘܗܠܝܢ ܡܠܟ̈ܬܐ ܐܝܬܝܗܘܢ ܛܒ̈ܐ.

ܕ. ܗܘ ܓܒܪܐ ܘܗܝ ܐܢܬܬܐ ܐܝܬܝܗܘܢ ܛܒ̈ܐ.

ܗ. ܗܘ ܛܠܝܐ ܪܡܐ. ܘܗܝ ܛܠܝܬܐ ܫܦܝܪܬܐ ܐܝܬܝܗܘܢ ܒܢ̈ܝܐ ܛܒ̈ܐ.

ܘ. ܗܢܘܢ ܣܘܣ̈ܝܐ ܪ̈ܘܪܒܐ ܘܗܠܝܢ ܣܘܣ̈ܝܬܐ ܪ̈ܘܪܒܬܐ.

Translate the following sentences into Aramaic and underscore the Aramaic demonstrative pronouns.

1- This is a holy book.

2- This good queen is kind.

3- These good girls; these good trees. (near)

4- That tall boy and that beautiful girl are good children.

5- Who is that boy? (distant)

6- Who is that queen? (distant)

7- Those fruits and those mares. (near)

REVIEW

A- Translate the following sentences into Aramaic.

1- These white books are holy.

2- This good man is kind.

3- That humble wife of the king.

4- These good fruits are sweet.

5- These men of peace are holy men.

6- Those beautiful black horses are large.

7- What is his good name?

8- Who is he?

9- How many apostles of Jesus?

10- Which house?

11- What is this?

12- Who wrote this book?

13- Which high mountains?

14- That boy is tall, that father is good, and that mother is nice.

15- Behold, (ܗܳܐ) the Lamb of God!

    B- Translate the following sentences into English.

1. ܫܡܶܗ ܫܰܦܺܝܪ.

CHAPTER FIVE
VERBS – AN INTRODUCTION

VERBS

AN INTRODUCTION

Reading

ܐ. ܐܡܪ ܝܫܘܥ : ܐܢܐ ܐܢܐ ܐܘܪܚܐ ܘܫܪܪܐ ܘܚܝܐ.

ܒ. ܒܝܬܠܚܡ ܡܕܝܢܬܐ ܐܝܬܝܗ ܐܬܪܗ ܕܝܫܘܥ ܦܪܘܩܢ.

ܓ. ܡܠܐܟܐ ܫܒܚܘ ܠܐܠܗܐ ܒܫܡܝܐ.

ܕ. ܬܠܡܝܕܐ ܕܝܫܘܥ ܐܝܬܝܗܘܢ ܟܘܟܒܐ ܕܡܪܘܡܐ.

ܗ. ܡܫܒܘܚܐ ܠܐܠܗܐ ܒܡܪܘܡܐ.

ܘ. ܫܘܒܚܐ ܠܐܠܗܐ ܠܥܠܡ.

ܙ. ܪܘܚܐ ܩܘܕܫܐ ܐܝܬܘܗܝ ܠܘܬ ܐܒܐ.

ܚ. ܐܠܗܐ ܒܪܐ ܠܥܠܡܐ ܒܡܠܬܗ ܕܡܫܒܚܐ.

ܛ. ܡܠܐܟܐ ܕܡܪܝܐ ܐܡܪ ܠܝܘܣܦ.

ܝ. ܟܘܟܒܐ ܪܒܐ ܢܦܠ ܡܢ ܫܡܝܐ.

VOCABULARY

1- Way   ܐܘܪܚܐ ܐܘܪܚܬܐ

2- There is / are   ܐܝܬ

3- Blessing   ܒܘܪܟܬܐ

4- Virgin, Virgins   ܒܬܘܠܬܐ ܒܬܘܠܬܐ

5- Life   ܚܝܐ

6- With, Toward   ܠܘܬ

7- There is not / are none   ܠܝܬ

8- Angel, Messenger   ܡܠܐܟܐ

9- Highest, high region   ܡܪܘܡܐ

10- Fell, will fall   ܢܦܠ ܢܦܠ

11- Made, will make   ܥܒܕ ܢܥܒܕ

12- Saved, will save   ܦܪܩ ܢܦܪܘܩ

13- Cross   ܨܠܝܒܐ

14- Killed, will kill   ܩܛܠ ܢܩܛܘܠ

15- Holy Spirit   ܪܘܚܐ ܕܩܘܕܫܐ

16- Praised, will praise   ܫܒܚ : ܢܫܒܚ

17- Praise, glory   ܫܘܒܚܐ

18- Heavens*   ܫܡܝܐ

19- Truth   ܫܪܪܐ

*NOTE: The Aramaic word ܫܡܝܐ may be translated in the singular – "heaven" or the plural – "heavens" The word also means "sky", "universe" and "cosmos".

1) **VERBS** - ܡܠܬܐ

    A verb is a word that expresses action or a state of being (by itself) without the use of another word. (NOTE: The word Miltha - ܡܠܬܐ is feminine when it means "verb"). Aramaic verbs are formed by radical letters (root letters):

Bilateral (two radicals) stood -   ܩܡ

Trilateral (three radicals) wrote -   ܟܬܒ

Quadrilateral (four radicals) interpreted -   ܦܫܩ

2) **USAGE OF VERBS**

    A. ACTIVE VOICE – He wrote   ܟܬܒ

    B. GENDER

        Masculine – He stands   ܩܐܡ

        Feminine – She stands   ܩܝܡܐ

    C. NUMBER

        Masculine Singular – He killed   ܩܛܠ

        Masculine Plural – They killed   ܩܛܠܘ

    D. PERSON – There are three persons.

        First Person – I write   ܟܬܒܢܐ

        Second Person – You write   ܟܬܒ ܐܢܬ

        Third Person – he writes   ܟܬܒ

E. MOODS

    Indicative – He wrote   ܟܬܒ

    Imperative – write!   ܟܬܘܒ

    Infinitive – To write   ܠܡܟܬܒ

F. TENSES There are three principal tenses.

    Past   ܐܢܐ ܕܟܬܒ - He wrote   ܟܬܒ

    Present   ܐܢܐ ܕܟܬܒ - He writes   ܟܬܒ

    Future   ܐܢܐ ܕܟܬܒ - He will write   ܢܟܬܘܒ

NOTE: Some grammatical textbooks classify the tenses in the following manner:
Perfect tense – complete (past).
Imperfect tense – incomplete (future).

In the ancient Aramaic language the present tense may also indicate the future (Imperfect). It does not have a clear future tense as in the Greek and Latin languages.

The Defective Verbs:

1) ܐܝܬ   To be or to have.

2) ܠܝܬ   Not to be or not to have.

These two particular verbs are called defective because they do not follow the usual form for conjugating.

THE VERB – <u>TO BE</u>   ܐܝܬ

Singular

First Person

M & F   - I am   ܐܢܐ ܐܝܬܝ

Second Person

M S   – You are   ܐܢܬ ܐܝܬܝܟ

F S	– You are	ܐܢܬܝ ܐܝܬܝܟܝ

Third Person

M S	– He is	ܗܘ ܐܝܬܘܗܝ
F S	– She is	ܗܝ ܐܝܬܝܗ

Plural

First Person

M & F	– We are	ܚܢܢ ܐܝܬܝܢ

Second Person

M P	– You are	ܐܢܬܘܢ ܐܝܬܝܟܘܢ
F P	– You are	ܐܢܬܝܢ ܐܝܬܝܟܝܢ

Third Person

M P	– They are	ܗܢܘܢ ܐܝܬܝܗܘܢ
F P	– They are	ܗܢܝܢ ܐܝܬܝܗܝܢ

THE VERB – TO HAVE   ܐܝܬ ܠܗ

Singular

First Person

M & F	– I have	ܐܝܬ ܠܝ

Second Person

M S	– You have	ܐܝܬ ܠܟ

F S	– You have	ܐܝܬ ܠܟܝ

Third Person

M S	– He has	ܐܝܬ ܠܗ
F S	– She has	ܐܝܬ ܠܗ̇

Plural

First Person

M & F	– We have	ܐܝܬ ܠܢ

Second Person

M P	– You have	ܐܝܬ ܠܟܘܢ
F P	– You have	ܐܝܬ ܠܟܝܢ

Third Person

M P	– They have	ܐܝܬ ܠܗܘܢ
F P	– They have	ܐܝܬ ܠܗܝܢ

THIRD VERB – <u>NOT TO BE</u> ܠܝܬ

Singular

First Person

M & F	– I am not	ܠܝܬܝ

Second Person

M S	– You are not	ܠܝܬܝܟ
F S	– You are not	ܠܝܬܝܟܝ

Third Person

M S	– He is not	ܠܰܝܬܰܘܗܝ
F S	– She is not	ܠܰܝܬܶܝܗ

Plural

First Person

M & F	– We are not	ܠܰܝܬܰܢ

Second Person

M P	– You are not	ܠܰܝܬܰܝܟܘܢ
F P	– You are not	ܠܰܝܬܰܝܟܶܝܢ

Third Person

M P	– They are not	ܠܰܝܬܰܝܗܘܢ
F P	– They are not	ܠܰܝܬܰܝܗܶܝܢ

THE VERB – <u>NOT TO HAVE</u>   ܠܰܝܬ ܠܶܗ

Singular

First Peron

M & F	– I do not have	ܠܰܝܬ ܠܺܝ

Second Person

M S	– You do not have	ܠܰܝܬ ܠܳܟ
F S	– You do not have	ܠܰܝܬ ܠܶܟܝ

Third Person

M S	– He does not have	ܠܰܝܬ ܠܶܗ

46

F S — She does not have ܠܝܗ ܠܗ̇

Plural
First Person

M & F — We do not have ܠܝܗ ܠܢ

Second Person

M P — You do not have ܠܝܗ ܠܟܘܢ

F P — You do not have ܠܝܗ ܠܟܝܢ

Third Person

M P — They do not have ܠܝܗ ܠܗܘܢ

F P — They do not have ܠܝܗ ܠܗܝܢ

REVIEW

1- Conjugate the verbs "to be" and "not to be" three times each.

A. To be ܝܬܒ

_____   _____   _____
_____   _____   _____
_____   _____   _____
_____   _____   _____
_____   _____   _____
_____   _____   _____
_____   _____   _____
_____   _____   _____

B. Not to be ܠܹܐ ܗܘܹܐ

2- Write the verbs "to have" and "not to have" three times each.

A. To have ܐܝܼܬ ܠܹܗ

B. Not to have ܠܹܗ ܠܹܗ

3- Translate the following sentences into Aramaic.

1) I am a good man.

2) You are a bad disciple.

3) She is a beautiful woman.

4) He is a tall boy.

5) Those black mountains are high.

6) He is not a bad boy.
_____

7) Thomas has a book.
_____

8) Mary does not have the holy books.
_____

9) The priest does not have a cross.
_____

10) I am not a king; I am a human being.
_____

4- Translate the following sentences into English.

ܐ. ܡܠܟܬܐ ܕܝܗܒ ܥܩܒܬܐ.

ܐ. _____

ܒ. ܩܕܝܫܐ ܐܠܗܐ ܕܝܗܘܒ ܕܘܡܟܠܗ ܦܪܝܫܐ.

ܒ. _____

ܓ. ܟܠܢܐ ܦܠܠܝܟܐ ܕܝܗܘܣܦ ܕܡܪ.

ܓ. _____

ܕ. ܐܝܬ ܠܝ ܐܣܦܪ.

ܕ. _____

ܗ. ܐܝܗܝ ܡܠܟܬ ܕܝܗܝ ܟܬܒܐ.

ܗ. _____

50

ه. ܡܠܟܬܐ ܐܝܬ ܠܗܘܢ ܚܕܐ ܒܪܬܐ.

ــ .ه

و. ܩܘܡ ܕܣܘܪܝܐ ܠܗ ܐܬܪܐ.

ــ .و

ح. ܒܘܒܚܘܢ ܕܐܬܪܐ ܕܝܗܒܗ ܣܓܝ.

ــ .ح

ط. ܐܬܗܪ ܕܝܗܒܝܢ ܒܘܬܠܬܐ.

ــ .ط

ي. ܐܬܗܘܢ ܕܝܗܒ ܠܗܘܢ ܪܒܐ ܘܒܪܬ.

ــ .ي

CHAPTER SIX
VERBS: Past Tense Indicative Mood (Perfect Tense)

Past Tense Indicative Mood (Perfect Tense)

Reading

ܐ. ܒܪܫܝܬ ܐܝܬܘܗܝ ܗܘܐ ܡܠܬܐ.

ܒ. ܘܗܘ ܡܠܬܐ ܐܝܬܘܗܝ ܗܘܐ ܠܘܬ ܐܠܗܐ.

ܓ. ܘܐܠܗܐ ܐܝܬܘܗܝ ܗܘ ܡܠܬܐ.

ܕ. ܗܢܐ ܐܝܬܘܗܝ ܗܘܐ ܒܪܫܝܬ ܠܘܬ ܐܠܗܐ.

ܗ. ܟܠ ܒܐܝܕܗ ܗܘܐ.

ܘ. ܒܗ ܚܝܐ ܗܘܐ.

ܙ. ܘܚܝܐ ܐܝܬܝܗܘܢ ܢܘܗܪܐ ܕܒܢܝܢܫܐ.

ܚ. ܗܢܐ ܐܬܐ ܠܣܗܕܘܬܐ.

ܛ. ܠܐ ܗܘ ܗܘܐ ܢܘܗܪܐ.

ܝ. ܘܡܠܬܐ ܒܣܪܐ ܗܘܐ.

VOCABULARY

He came	ܐܬܐ
Mankind, Humankind	ܒܢܝܢܫܐ
Flesh, Meat, Physical form	ܒܣܪܐ
Witness	ܣܗܕܘܬܐ

The usual form of the verb before conjugation is always put in the third person masculine singular. A square dot placed under and between the first and second consonants of the verb indicates the past tense.

Example :–

He wrote ܟܬܒ (Past Tense)

He killed ܩܛܠ (Past Tense) or He saved ܦܪܩ (Past Tense)

The Conjugation of the verbs in the Past Tense, Active Voice.

THE VERB –   TO WRITE   ܟܬܒ

Singular

First Person

M & F   - I wrote   (ܶܬ݇)   ܟܶܬܒܶܬ

Second Person

M S   - You wrote   (ܬ݇)   ܟܬܰܒܬ

F S   - You wrote   (ܬܝ݇)   ܟܬܰܒܬܝ

Third Person

M S   - He wrote   (—)   ܟܬܰܒ

F S   - She wrote   (ܰܬ݇)   ܟܶܬܒܰܬ

Plural

First Person

M & F   - We wrote   (ܢ) or (ܢ݇)   ܟܬܰܒܢ or ܟܬܰܒܢܢ

Second Person

M P   - You wrote   (ܬܘܢ)   ܟܬܒܬܘܢ

F P   - You wrote   (ܬܝܢ)   ܟܬܒܬܝܢ

Third Person

M P   - They wrote   (ܘܢ) or (ܘ)   ܟܬܒܘܢ or ܟܬܒܘ

F P   - They wrote   (ܝܢ) or (ܬܝܢ) ܟܬܒܝ or ܟܬܒܬܝܢ

THE VERB - TO SAVE   ܦܪܩ

Singular

First Person

M & F   - I saved   (ܝܬ)   ܦܪܩܝܬ

Second Person:

M S   - He saved   (ܬ)   ܦܪܩܬ

F S   - She saved   (ܬܝ)   ܦܪܩܬܝ

Third Person:

M S   - He saved   (ــ)   ܦܪܩ

F S   - She saved   (ܬ)   ܦܪܩܬ

Plural

First Person

M & F   - We saved   (ܢ) or (ܝܢ)   ܦܪܩܢ or ܦܪܩܝܢ

Second Person

M P - You saved (ܬܘܢ) ܩܲܕܸܡܬܘܢ

F P - You saved (ܬܹܝܢ) ܩܲܕܸܡܬܹܝܢ

Third Person

M P - They saved ! (ܘ) or (ܘܢ) ܩܲܕܸܡܘ or ܩܲܕܸܡܘܢ

F P - They saved ! (ܝ) or (ܢ) ܩܲܕܸܡܝ or ܩܲܕܸܡܢ

NOTE: In the second person feminine plural singular – Taw Yodh ܬܝ , the Yodh ܝ is written but it is not pronounced. The same rule applies to the third person masculine plural. The Waw ܘ is written but it is not pronounced. Also, the Siyame ¨ must be added in all verbs in the third person feminine plural only.

The Defective Verbs - ܗܘܐ and ܠܒܐ in the past tense.

THE VERB – TO BE ܗܘܐ PAST TENSE – WAS.

Singular

First Person

M & F – I was ܗܘܝܬ ܐܢܐ

Second Person

M S – You were ܗܘܝܬ ܐܢܬ

F S – You were ܗܘܝܬܝ ܐܢܬܝ

Third Person

M S — He was ܐܝܼܬ݂ܘܵܗܝ ܗܘܵܐ

F S — She was ܐܝܼܬ݂ܝܗ ܗܘܵܗ

Plural

First Person

M & F — We were ܐܝܼܬ݂ܝܼܢ ܗܘܲܝܢ

Second Person

M P — You were ܐܝܼܬ݂ܝܼܟ݂ܘܿܢ ܗܘܲܝܬܘܿܢ

F P — You were ܐܝܼܬ݂ܝܼܟܹܝܢ ܗܘܲܝܬܹܝܢ

Third Person

M P — They were ܐܝܼܬ݂ܝܗܘܿܢ ܗܘܵܘ

F P — They were ܐܝܼܬ݂ܝܗܹܝܢ ܗܘܲܝ

THE VERB – NOT TO BE ܠܝܬ PAST TENSE – WAS NOT.

Singular

First Person

M & F — I was not ܗܘܹܝܬ ܠܝܬ

Second Person

M S — You were not ܠܝܬ ܗܘܲܝܬ

F S — You were not ܠܝܬ ܗܘܲܝܬܝ

Third Person

M S   - He was not   ܠܶܐ ܗܘܳܐ ܗܘܽ

F S   - She was not   ܠܶܐ ܗܘܳܬ݂ ܗܺܝ

Plural

First Person

M & F   - We were not   ܠܶܐ ܗܘܰܝܢ

Second Person

M P   - You were not   ܠܶܐ ܗܘܰܝܬܘܢ

F P   - You were not   ܠܶܐ ܗܘܰܝܬܶܝܢ

Third Person

M P   - They were not   ܠܶܐ ܗܘܰܘ

F P   - They were not   ܠܶܐ ܗܘܰܝ

THE VERB – TO HAVE   ܐܺܝܬ݂ ܠܺܝ   PAST TENSE – HAD

Singular

First Person

M & F   - I had   ܐܺܝܬ݂ ܗܘܳܐ ܠܺܝ

Second Person

M S   - You had   ܐܺܝܬ݂ ܗܘܳܐ ܠܳܟ݂

F S   - You had   ܐܺܝܬ݂ ܗܘܳܐ ܠܶܟ݂ܝ

Third Person

M S   - He had   ܐܝܬ ܗܘܵܐ ܠܹܗ

F S   - She had   ܐܝܬ ܗܘܵܐ ܠܵܗܿ

Plural

First Person

M & F   - We had   ܐܝܬ ܗܘܵܐ ܠܲܢ

Second Person

M P   - You had   ܐܝܬ ܗܘܵܐ ܠܟ݂ܘܿܢ

F P   - You had   ܐܝܬ ܗܘܵܐ ܠܟܹܝܢ

Third Person

M P   - They had   ܐܝܬ ܗܘܵܐ ܠܗܘܿܢ

F P   - They had   ܐܝܬ ܗܘܵܐ ܠܗܹܝܢ

THE VERB – NOT TO HAVE ܠܲܝܬ ܠܹܗ - PAST TENSE – DID NOT HAVE

Singular

First Person

M & F   - I didn't have   ܠܲܝܬ ܗܘܵܐ ܠܝܼ

Second Person

M S   - You didn't have   ܠܲܝܬ ܗܘܵܐ ܠܘܼܟ݂

F S   - You didn't have   ܠܲܝܬ ܗܘܵܐ ܠܹܟ݂ܝ

Third Person

M S	- He didn't have	ܠܼܗ ܗܵܘܹܐ ܠܸܗ
F S	- She didn't have	ܠܼܗ ܗܵܘܹܐ ܠܵܗ

Plural

First Person

M & F	- We didn't have	ܠܼܗ ܗܵܘܹܐ ܠܲܢ

Second Person

M P	- You didn't have	ܠܼܗ ܗܵܘܹܐ ܠܵܟ݂ܘܿܢ
F P	- You didn't have	ܠܼܗ ܗܵܘܹܐ ܠܵܟܹܝܢ

Third Person

M P	- They didn't have	ܠܼܗ ܗܵܘܹܐ ܠܗܘܿܢ
F P	- They didn't have	ܠܼܗ ܗܵܘܹܐ ܠܗܹܝܢ

REVIEW

1- Conjugate the following verbs in the past tense.

ܚܵܙܹܒ݂	ܦܵܬܹܚ	ܢܵܦܹܠ
_____	_____	_____
_____	_____	_____
_____	_____	_____
_____	_____	_____

2- Translate the following sentences into Aramaic.

1) The apostles wrote the holy books.

2) The disciples of Jesus were good men.

3) Thomas is an apostle of truth.

4) Those good men were men of God.

5) Our women were beautiful and are beautiful this day.

6) The bear killed those red mares.

7) God's angels are in heaven and on earth.

8) The cross of Jesus is a blessing.

9) Jesus's mother's name is Mary.

____

10) Jesus said, "I am the way, the truth and the life ".

____

11) We have five holy books at home.

____

12) I had the holy books in the temple.

____

13) John wasn't in the house. I was in the house.

____

14) He said the words and they wrote the words in that large book.

____

3- Translate the following sentences into English.

ܐ. ܫܘܒܚܐ ܠܐܒܐ ܘܠܒܪܐ ܘܠܪܘܚܐ ܩܘܕܫܐ.

ܐ. ____

ܒ. ܐܠܗܐ ܐܝܬܘܗܝ ܚܘܒܐ.

ܒ. ____

ܓ. ܡܠܟܐ ܕܡܕܝܢܐ ܐܙܠ ܠܒܝܬܐ ܕܡܕܝܢܬܐ ܘܐܡܪ ܠܗ: ܫܠܡ ܠܟܝ ܡܕܝܢܬܐ

ܓ. ____

ܕ. ܝܫܘܥ ܐܝܬܘܗܝ ܡܠܟܗ ܕܐܠܗܐ.

ܕ. ____

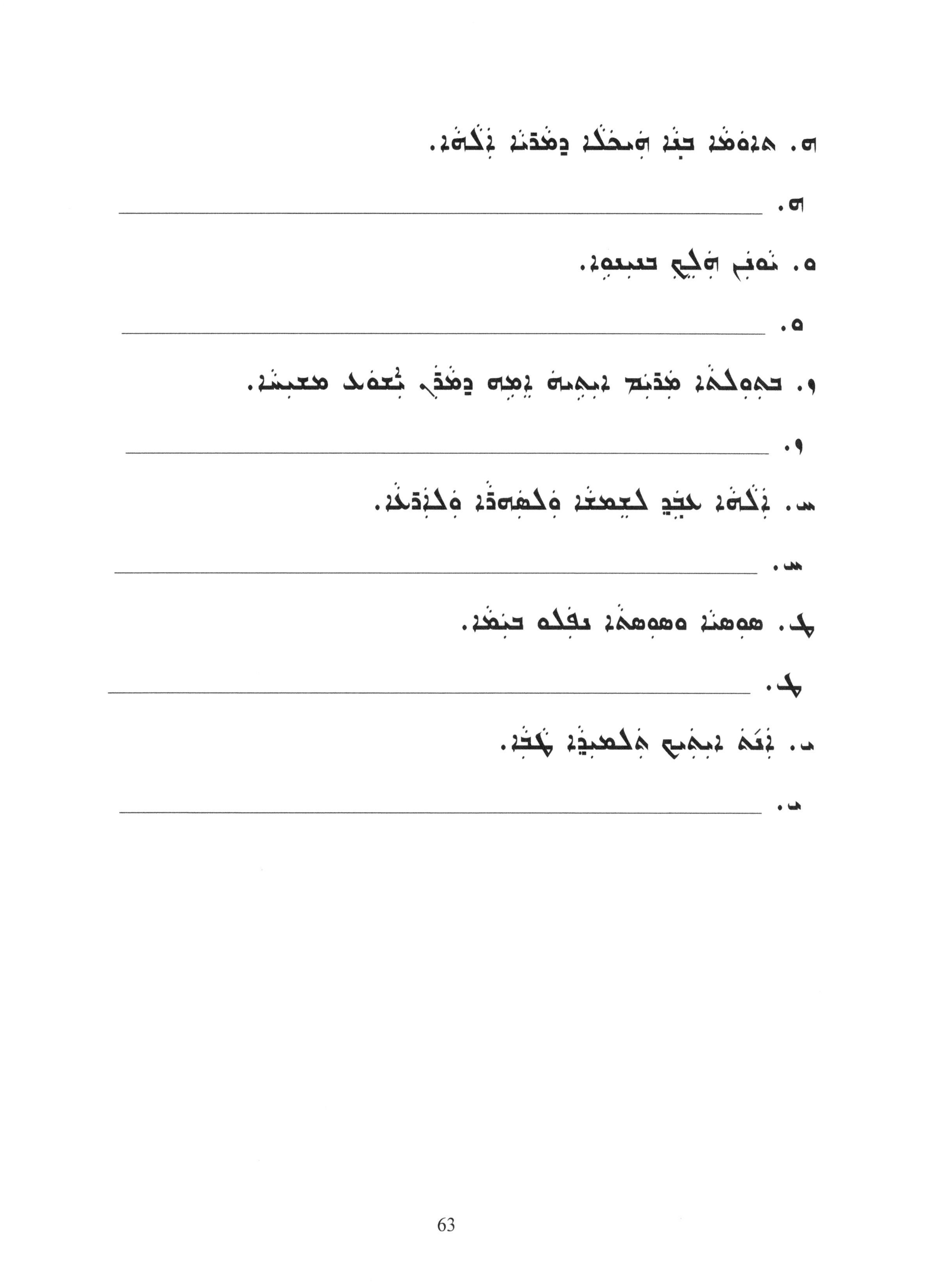

CHAPTER SEVEN

PRESENT TENSE INDICATIVE MOOD

PRESENT TENSE INDICATIVE MOOD

Reading

ܐ. ܐܬܐ ܝܘܚܢܢ ܡܥܡܕܢܐ ܘܡܟܪܙ ܗܘܐ ܒܚܘܪܒܐ ܕܝܗܘܕ.

ܒ. ܓܝܣܐ ܠܐ ܐܬܐ.

ܓ. ܘܩܥܐ ܝܘܚܢܢ ܘܐܡܪ: ܗܢܐ ܗܘ ܗܘ.

ܕ. ܘܢܦܩ ܝܫܘܥ ܠܚܘܪܒܐ. ܘܥܡܪ ܬܡܢ ܥܡ ܬܠܡܝܕܘܗܝ.

ܗ. ܐܡܪ ܠܗ ܦܝܠܝܦܘܣ.

ܘ. ܐܟܠ ܝܫܘܥ ܘܡܒܪܟ ܠܚܡܐ

ܙ. ܐܡܝܢ ܐܡܝܢ ܐܡܪ ܐܢܐ ܠܟܘܢ.

ܚ. ܕܡܢ ܕܠܐ ܥܐܠ ܡܢ ܬܪܥܐ ܗܘ ܓܝܣܐ ܗܘ.

ܛ. ܐܡܪ ܐܢܐ ܠܟܘܢ : ܝܗܒ ܐܢܐ ܠܚܡܐ ܕܚܝܐ.

ܝ. ܝܗܒ ܐܢܐ ܕܝܢܐ ܛܒܐ

VOCABULARY

Blessed	ܡܒܪܟ
Bandit	ܓܝܣܐ
Desert, Wilderness	ܚܘܪܒܐ
Judah (Judea)	ܝܗܘܕ

Sat down	ܝܬܒ
Preaching, Declaring	ܡܟܪܙܘ
Anyone	ܐܢܫ
Baptist, Baptizer	ܡܥܡܕܢܐ
Enter	ܥܘܠ
Philip	ܦܝܠܝܦܘܣ
Called (Cried out)	ܩܥܐ
Shepherd	ܪܥܝܐ
Received (took)	ܩܒܠ
There (adv. Of place)	ܬܡܢ

A Few General Rules

    There are many rules for forming the present tense. For beginners the following rules are sufficient.

  A. Bilateral verbs are formed in the following manner:

    To stand (stood) ܩܡ the letter Alap ܐ is added as a medial letter.

    - ܩܐܡ = ܡ + ܩ + ܐ   Standing (present tense or present participle).

  B. Trilateral verbs are formed in the following manner:

    A Zqapa is added on the first radical and a Pthaha or a Zlama Qashya may be added on the second radical.

    To open (opened) ܦܬܚ   opens or is opening ܦܬܚ

To kill (killed) ܩܛܶܠ kills or is killing ܩܳܛܶܠ

C. Quadrilateral verbs are formed in the following manner:

Non – vocalized Meem ܡ is prefixed to the past tense of the verb.

To disciple (disciple) ܬܰܠܡܶܕ disciples or is disciple ܡܬܰܠܡܶܕ

D. When conjugating the present tense, subject pronouns (personal pronouns) are used and is some cases they are suffixed to the verb.

REMINDER: The present tense indicates the following:

1) I write
2) I do write
3) I am writing

THE VERB – TO WRITE ܟܳܬܶܒ

Singular

First Person

M S   – I write   ܟܳܬܶܒ ܐܢܳܐ

F S   – I write   ܟܳܬܒܳܐ ܐܢܳܐ

Second Person

M S   – You write   ܟܳܬܶܒ ܐܰܢ݈ܬ

F S   - You write   ܟܳܬܒܳܐ ܐܰܢ݈ܬܝ

Third Person

M S   - He writes   ܟܳܬܶܒ

F S   – She writes   ܟܳܬܒܳܐ

Plural

First Person

M S   – We write   ܟܵܬܒܝܼܢ

F S   – We write   ܟܵܬܬܝܼܢ

Second Person

M S   – You write   ܟܵܬܒܝܼܬܘܿܢ

F S   - You write   ܟܵܬܬܝܼܬܘܿܢ

Third Person

M S   - They write   ܟܵܬܒܝܼ

F S   – They write   ܟܵܬܬܝܼ

NOTE: The present tense takes a large point over the middle letter of the verb when conjugating.

Example   ܥܵܒܸܕ   (See Ch. 2, P 78, rule A, Book I- "In verbs").

REVIEW

1- Conjugate the following verbs in the present tense.

       ܟܵܬܒ   ܥܵܒܸܕ   ܢܵܚܹܬ

_____   _____   _____

_____   _____   _____

_____   _____   _____

_____   _____   _____

2- Translate the following sentences into English.

܂. ܗܘܗܬܝܼ ܕܘܚܶܬ ܢܰܘܠܒܝ ܠܬܕܝܓܝܘܗܝ܂

2. _____

ܒ. ܥܠܝܬܐ ܐܓܠܒܝ ܒܰܚ ܢܥܘܕ܂

ܒ. _____

ܓ. ܚܕܝܬ ܗܘܠܓܝ ܕܘܝܚܠܕ܂

ܓ. _____

ܕ. ܝܝܬ ܡܢܝܚܣܝ ܠܐܠܟܢܝ

ܕ. _____

69

ܗ. ܗܘܝ ܦܬܚܝܢ ܬܪܥܘܗܝ ܘܟܘܘܘܗܝ.

ܗ. ______________________________

ܘ. ܢܬܘܒ ܩܕܡ ܠܐܠܗܐ ܡܢ ܚܛܝܬܐ.

ܘ. ______________________________

ܙ. ܬܠܓܐ ܢܦܝܠ ܥܠ ܛܘܪܐ.

ܙ. ______________________________

ܚ. ܕܝܟܐ ܩܥܐ ܨܦܪܐ.

ܚ. ______________________________

ܛ. ܡܠܦܢܐ ܐܡܪ: ܐܢܬܘܢ ܐܝܬܘܢ ܬܠܡܝܕܐ ܛܒܐ.

ܛ. ______________________________

ܝ. ܠܒܝ ܡܫܒܚ ܠܡܪܝܐ.

ܝ. ______________________________

CHAPTER EIGHT

Verbs: The Future Tense Indicative Mood (Imperfect Tense)

The Future Tense Indicative Mood (Imperfect Tense)

Reading

ܐ. ܘܐܡܪ ܐܠܗܐ: ܢܗܘܐ ܢܘܗܪܐ ܘܗܘܐ ܢܘܗܪܐ.

ܒ. ܘܩܪܐ ܐܠܗܐ ܠܢܘܗܪܐ ܐܝܡܡܐ: ܘܠܚܫܘܟܐ ܩܪܐ ܠܠܝܐ.

ܓ. ܘܐܡܪ ܡܪܝܐ ܠܐܒܪܡ: ܙܠ ܠܟ ܡܢ ܐܪܥܟ ܠܐܪܥܐ ܕܐܚܘܝܟ.

ܕ. ܘܐܥܒܕܟ ܠܥܡܐ ܪܒܐ: ܘܐܒܪܟܟ ܘܐܪܒܐ ܫܡܟ.

ܗ. ܘܐܙܠ ܠܘܛ ܥܡܗ.

ܘ. ܐܡܪ ܠܗ ܝܫܘܥ: ܐܡܝܢ ܐܡܝܢ ܐܡܪ ܐܢܐ ܠܟܘܢ: ܕܡܢ ܗܫܐ ܬܚܙܘܢ ܫܡܝܐ ܕܦܬܝܚܝܢ.

ܙ. ܐܡܪ ܠܗ ܦܝܠܝܦܘܣ: ܬܐ ܘܚܙܝ.

ܚ. ܪܘܪܒܢ ܡܢ ܗܠܝܢ ܬܚܙܐ.

ܛ. ܕܠܡܐ ܬܥܠܘܢ ܠܢܣܝܘܢܐ.

ܝ. ܛܘܒܝܗܘܢ ܠܐܝܠܝܢ ܕܕܟܝܢ ܒܠܒܗܘܢ . ܕܗܢܘܢ ܢܚܙܘܢ ܠܐܠܗܐ.

VOCABULARY

I will bless you	ܐܒܪܟܟ
I will make great	ܐܪܒܐ
I will show you	ܐܚܘܝܟ

I will make from you	ܐܥܒܕܟ
Amen	ܐܡܝܢ
I will go	ܐܙܠ
Pure ones	ܕܟܝܐ
Perhaps	ܕܠܡܐ
Now	ܗܫܐ
Go, Depart, Leave	ܙܠ
Darkness	ܚܫܘܟܐ
Happy, Blessed	ܛܘܒܝܗܘܢ
Night	ܠܠܝܐ
Let be	ܢܗܘܐ
They shall see	ܢܚܙܘܢ
People, Nation	ܥܡܐ
Philip	ܦܝܠܝܦܘܣ
Opening	ܦܬܚ
He called, named	ܩܪܐ
Come	ܬܐ

A Few General Rules

There are many rules for forming the future tense. For beginners the following rules are sufficient.

A- Bilateral verbs that carry a Zqapa ܰ become Rwasa ܘ

Example: to stand (stood) ܩܡ I will stand ܢܩܘܡ

NOTE: (Alap ܐ is used for the first person singular) but, when the verb carries a Pthaha ܰ some bilateral verbs remain the same and others become Rwaha ܘ

Examples: Desired ܒܥܐ , I will desire ܢܒܥܐ (NOTE: The Pthaha did not change).

Plundered ܒܙ , I will plunder ܢܒܘܙ (NOTE: The Pthaha becomes a Rwaha).

B- Trilateral verbs may become a Rwaha ܘ or remain the same.

Example: was jealous ܣܥܡ , I will be jealous ܢܣܥܡ (NOTE: There is no change in the verb "jealous").

Killed ܩܛܠ , I will kill ܢܩܛܘܠ (NOTE: The Pthaha becomes a Rwaha).

C- Quadrilateral verbs make no changes in their root.

Example: Interpreted ܦܫܩ , I will interpret ܢܦܫܩ

THE VERB - TO SAVE ܦܪܩ

Singular

First Person

M & F – I will save ܢܦܪܩ

Second Person

M S   – You will save   ܬܸܦܪܘܿܩ

F S   -You will save   ܬܸܦܪܩܝܼܢ

Third Person

M S   - He will save   ܒܸܦܪܘܿܩ

F S   – She will save   ܬܸܦܪܘܿܩ

Plural

First Person

M & F   – We will save   ܒܸܦܪܘܿܩ

Second Person

M P   – You will save   ܬܸܦܪܩܘܼܢ

F P   -You will save   ܬܸܦܪܩܝܼܢ

Third Person

M P   - They will save   ܒܸܦܪܩܘܼܢ

F P   – They will save   ܒܸܦܪܩܝܼܢ

The Defective Verbs - ܐܝܼܬ and ܗܘܹܐ in the future tense.

THE VERB – TO BE ܐܝܼܬ FUTRUE TENSE – WILL BE.

Singular

First Person

M & F   – I will be   ܐܵܘܸܢ ܐܝܼܬ

75

Second Person

| M S | – You will be | ܗܘܿܝܬ ܠܒܵܝܬ |
| F S | – You will be | ܗܘܿܝܬܝ ܠܒܵܝܬܐ |

Third Person

| M S | – He will be | ܗܘܿܝ ܠܒܵܝܬܗ |
| F S | – She will be | ܗܘܿܝܐ ܠܒܵܝܬܗ |

Plural

First Person

| M & F | – We will be | ܗܘܿܝܚ ܠܒܵܝܬ |

Second Person

| M P | – You will be | ܗܘܿܝܬܘܢ ܠܒܵܝܬ |
| F P | – You will be | ܗܘܿܝܬܝܢ ܠܒܵܝܬ |

Third Person

| M P | – They will be | ܗܘܿܘܢ ܠܒܵܝܬܗܘܢ |
| F P | – They will be | ܗܘܿܝܢ ܠܒܵܝܬܗܝܢ |

THE VERB - NOT TO BE ܠܝܬ FUTURE TENSE – WILL NOT BE

Singular

First Person

| M & F | – I will not be | ܗܘܿܝܢ ܠܠܒܵܝܬ |

Second Person

M S – You will not be ܬܗܘܐ ܠܝܬܟ

F S -You will not be ܬܗܘܝܢ ܠܝܬܟܝ

Third Person

M S - He will not be ܢܗܘܐ ܠܝܬܗ

F S – She will not be ܬܗܘܐ ܠܝܬܗ̇

__Plural__

First Person

M & F – We will not be ܢܗܘܐ ܠܝܬܢ

Second Person

M P – You will not be ܬܗܘܘܢ ܠܝܬܟܘܢ

F P -You will not be ܬܗܘܝܢ ܠܝܬܟܝܢ

Third Person

M P - They will not be ܢܗܘܘܢ ܠܝܬܗܘܢ

F P – They will not be ܬܗܘܝܢ ܠܝܬܗܝܢ

THE VERB – TO HAVE ܐܝܬ ܠܗ FUTURE TENSE – WILL HAVE

__Singular__

First Person

M & F – I will have ܐܗܘܐ ܐܝܬ ܠܝ

Second Person

M S   – You will have   ܗܵܘܹܐ ܒܝܼܬ ܠܘܼܟ݂

F S   _You will have   ܗܵܘܹܐ ܒܝܼܬ ܠܵܟ݂ܝ

Third Person

M S   - He will have   ܗܵܘܹܐ ܒܝܼܬ ܠܹܗ

F S   – She will have   ܗܵܘܹܐ ܒܝܼܬ ܠܵܗ̇

Plural

First Person

M & F   – We will have   ܗܵܘܹܐ ܒܝܼܬ ܠܲܢ

Second Person

M P   – You will have   ܗܵܘܹܐ ܒܝܼܬ ܠܵܘܟ݂ܘܿܢ

F P   -You will have   ܗܵܘܹܐ ܒܝܼܬ ܠܵܟ݂ܝܢ

Third Person

M P   - They will have   ܗܵܘܹܐ ܒܝܼܬ ܠܗܘܿܢ

F P   – They will have   ܗܵܘܹܐ ܒܝܼܬ ܠܗܹܝܢ

THE VERB – NOT TO HAVE   ܠܹܗ ܠܲܝܬ   **FUTURE TENSE – WILL NOT HAVE**

Singular

First Person

M & F   – I will not have   ܠܹܐ ܗܵܘܹܐ ܠܝܼ

Second Person

M S   – You will not have   ܗܘܹܐ ܠܹܗ ܠܘܼܟ݂

F S   – You will not have   ܗܘܹܐ ܠܹܗ ܠܵܟ݂ܝ

Third Person

M S   – He will not have   ܗܘܹܐ ܠܹܗ ܠܹܗ

F S   – She will not have   ܗܘܹܐ ܠܹܗ ܠܵܗ̇

Plural

First Person

M & F   – We will not have   ܗܘܹܐ ܠܹܗ ܠܲܢ

Second Person

M P   – You will not have   ܗܘܹܐ ܠܹܗ ܠܵܘܟ݂ܘܿܢ

F P   – You will not have   ܗܘܹܐ ܠܹܗ ܠܵܟ݂ܹܝܢ

Third Person

M P   – They will not have   ܗܘܹܐ ܠܹܗ ܠܗܘܿܢ

F P   – They will not have   ܗܘܹܐ ܠܹܗ ܠܗܹܝܢ

REVIEW

1- Conjugate the following verbs in the future tense.

ܟܵܬܹܒ݂	ܙܵܪܘܿܥ	ܦܵܪܹܩ
I will write	I will plant	I will save

_____ _____ _____

2- Translate the following sentences into Aramaic.

1) The snow will fall on the house.

_____

2) The men will praise God in his holy temple.

_____

3) The bear will kill the man.

_____

4) The good men will write in the holy books.

_____

5) The apostle Thomas will build the house of God.

_____

6) You (F P) will plunder the house of the evil man.

7) The bull will kill the horse.

8) The Holy Spirit will save friends of the apostles.

9) The hand of the lord God will fall on the people.

10) The mother will save her daughter from the evil image.

3- Translate the following sentences into English.

ܐ. ܢܦܩܘܢ ܒܢ̈ܝܟ ܠܚܩܠܐ.

ܐ.

ܒ. ܩܛܠܐ ܝܘܕܥ ܣܓܝܐ.

ܒ.

ܓ. ܢܚܘܢ ܥܒܕܘܗܝ ܕܓܒܪܐ ܛܒܐ.

ܓ.

ܕ. ܝܥܪ̈ܐ ܣܢܝܩܝܢ ܡܢ ܐܬܪܘ̈ܬܝܗܘܢ.

ܕ. _____

ܗ. ܥܠܝܡܬܐ ܚܕܐ ܗܘܬ ܕܡܨܠܝܐ ܠܥܠܝܗ̇ ܕܢܐܪܐ.

ܗ. _____

ܘ. ܢܚܦܘܕ ܝܩܘܪܐ ܚܢܘܬܐ ܗܠܝܢܐ.

ܘ. _____

ܙ. ܩܕܡܐ ܝܥܪܝ ܢܐܬܐ ܠܬܪܣܩܘܗܝ

ܙ. _____

ܚ. ܡܠܐܟܐ ܕܡܪܢ ܢܐܪܟܠ ܥܪܐ.

ܚ. _____

ܛ. ܩܕܡܐ ܝܩܕܝܢ ܡܢ ܚܝܥܐ.

ܛ. _____

ܝ. ܐܪܐ ܝܗܒܘܬ ܥܩܢܘܬܝ ܢܥܝܐ.

CHAPTER NINE

VERBS: THE IMPERATIVE AND INFINITIVE MOODS

THE IMPERATIVE AND INFINITIVE MOODS

Reading
The LORD'S PRAYER
Mathew 6:9-13

ܐܒܘܢ ܕܒܫܡܝܐ. ܢܬܩܕܫ ܫܡܟ.

ܬܐܬܐ ܡܠܟܘܬܟ. ܢܗܘܐ ܨܒܝܢܟ. ܐܝܟܢܐ ܕܒܫܡܝܐ ܐܦ ܒܐܪܥܐ.

ܗܒ ܠܢ ܠܚܡܐ ܕܣܘܢܩܢܢ ܝܘܡܢܐ.

ܘܫܒܘܩ ܠܢ ܚܘܒܝܢ. ܐܝܟܢܐ ܕܐܦ ܚܢܢ ܫܒܩܢ ܠܚܝܒܝܢ.

ܘܠܐ ܬܥܠܢ ܠܢܣܝܘܢܐ. ܐܠܐ ܦܨܢ ܡܢ ܒܝܫܐ. ܡܛܠ ܕܕܝܠܟ ܐܦ ܡܠܟܘܬܐ.

ܘܚܝܠܐ ܘܬܫܒܘܚܬܐ. ܠܥܠܡ ܥܠܡܝܢ.

ܐܡܝܢ ✝

THE BEATITUDES
Matthew 5:3-9

܂. ܛܘܒܝܗܘܢ ܠܡܣܟܢܐ ܒܪܘܚ. ܕܕܝܠܗܘܢ ܐܦ ܡܠܟܘܬܐ ܕܫܡܝܐ.

܂. ܛܘܒܝܗܘܢ ܠܐܒܝܠܐ. ܕܗܢܘܢ ܢܬܒܝܐܘܢ.

܂. ܛܘܒܝܗܘܢ ܠܡܟܝܟܐ. ܕܗܢܘܢ ܢܐܪܬܘܢ ܐܪܥܐ.

܂. ܛܘܒܝܗܘܢ ܠܐܝܠܝܢ ܕܟܦܢܝܢ ܘܨܗܝܢ ܠܟܐܢܘܬܐ. ܕܗܢܘܢ ܢܣܒܥܘܢ.

ܕ. ܛܘܒܝܗܘܢ ܠܡܪ̈ܚܡܢܐ ܕܥܠܝܗܘܢ ܢܗܘܘܢ ܪ̈ܚܡܐ.

ܗ. ܛܘܒܝܗܘܢ ܠܐܝܠܝܢ ܕܕܟܝܢ ܒܠܒܗܘܢ. ܕܗܢܘܢ ܢܚܙܘܢ ܠܐܠܗܐ.

ܘ. ܛܘܒܝܗܘܢ ܠܐܝܬܘ̈ܗܝ ܥܠܡܐ. ܕܗܢܘܢ ܕܐܠܗܐ ܢܬܩܪܘܢ.

VOCABULARY

Mourners	ܐܒܝ̈ܠܐ
Even as	ܐܝܟܢܐ
But	ܐܠܐ
Also	ܐܦ
Give	ܗܒ
Debts, Offenses	ܚܘܒܐ
Justice, Righteousness	ܟܐܢܘܬܐ
Hungering (ones)	ܟܦܢܝܢ
Meek, Lowly (ones)	ܡܟܝ̈ܟܐ
Poor (ones)	ܡܣ̈ܟܢܐ
Merciful, Compassionate (ones)	ܡܪ̈ܚܡܢܐ
They shall inherit	ܢܐܪܬܘܢ
They shall be satisfied	ܢܣܒܥܘܢ

Temptation	ܢܸܣܝܘܿܢܵܐ
They shall be consoled	ܢܸܬܒ݂ܲܝܐܘܿܢ
Let be holy	ܢܸܬܩܲܕܲܫ
Our needs	ܣܢܝܼܩܘܵܬܲܢ
Peacemakers	ܥܵܒ݂ܕܲܝ ܫܠܵܡܵܐ
Deliver us	ܦܲܨܵܢ
Will, Wish, Desire	ܨܸܒ݂ܝܵܢܵܐ
Thirsting (ones)	ܨܲܗܝܹ̈ܐ
Forgive	ܫܒ݂ܘܿܩ
Let come	ܬܹܐܬܹܐ
(us) enter	ܬܲܥܠܲܢ

The Imperative Mood

(Commands)

Strong Verbs Only

A- Commanding verbs (imperatives) use the second person singular and plural only.

B- The Stem of the imperative is the second person masculine singular.

  Ex. : Wrote ܟܬܲܒ݂

C- The imperative is formed from the perfect stem (3 m.s) with or without vowel changes. There are five classification in the imperative depending on the change of vowels and are as follows:

Class	Perfect	Vowel	Changed to	Imperative
1-	ܟܬܲܒ݂	ܲ	ܘ݁	Write ܟܬ݂ܘ݁ܒ݂
2-	ܦܬܲܚ	ܲ	ܲ	Open - ܦܬܲܚ (no change)
3-	ܪܚܸܡ	ܸ	ܸ	Love ܪܚܸܡ
4-	ܫܬܸܩ	ܸ	ܘ݁	Keep quiet - ܫܬ݂ܘ݁ܩ
5-	ܠܚܹܝܡ	ܸ	ܸ	Work - ܠܚܹܝܡ

Conjugation

Wrote -	ܟܬܲܒ݂	He was silent (Quiet) -	ܫܬܸܩ
Write M S -	ܟܬ݂ܘ݁ܒ݂	Be quiet M S -	ܫܬ݂ܘ݁ܩ
Write F S -	ܟܬ݂ܘ݁ܒ݂ܝ	Be Silent F S -	ܫܬ݂ܘ݁ܩܝ
Write M P -	ܟܬ݂ܘܒܘܢ	Be Silent M P -	ܫܬ݂ܘܩܘܢ
Write F P -	ܟܬ݂ܘ݁ܒ݂ܹܝܢ ܟܬ݂ܘ݁ܒ݂ܬܸܢ	Be Silent F P -	ܫܬ݂ܘ݁ܩܹܝܢ ܫܬ݂ܘ݁ܩܬܸܢ

NOTE: In the strong verbs (Imperative) the formed by radical is always hard; and the second and third radicals are always soft.

The Infinitive Mood

The infinitive mood (to) is formed by prefixing ܡ or ܠܡ to the stem of the perfect 3. M. as in ܟܬܒ and means "to write". When the Meem (ܡ) is prefixed it takes the Zlama Psheeqa ܡܶ. ܠܡܶ or the Zlama Qasha ܡܷ ، ܠܡܷ . The Pthaha ܰ is retained on the stem. If the stem doesn't have a Pthaha than that particular vowel must be changed to a Pthaha ܰ only when forming an infinitive – (exception is a concave verb). The infinitive has no person, gender or number. When a ܠܡ is prefixed to the stem of a verb, it is in the construct (Cons). State. When a ܡ is prefixed to the stem of a verb, it is in the absolute (Abs). state.

Prefix	Stem	Infinitive		
ܡ	ܫܲܠܡܸܕ	To complete -	ܡܫܲܠܡܸܕ	, Abs.
ܠܡ	ܫܲܠܡܸܕ	To perfect -	ܠܡܫܲܠܡܸܕ	, Cons.
ܡ	ܣܦܸܕ	To envy -	ܡܣܦܸܕ	, Abs.
ܠܡ	ܫܲܠܡܸܕ	To envy -	ܠܡܣܦܸܕ	, Cons.

Exercises

A- Translate the following sentences into Aramaic.
  1- My father said to me, "Be silent".

  2- You (S M) write the holy words of God in the book of truth.

  _____

3- The Lord said to Mary, "Open the book of life".

4- For me, to work is to write.

5- Your will is life and truth.

6- And John said, "Let your will be done!"

7- Girls, "Be silent!"

8- The teacher said to his students, "Work and be quiet".

9- Deliver us from evil.

10- Blessed are good men for theirs is the kingdom of God.

Dictionary

Aramaic to English

	ܒ
August	ܐܳܒ
Mourners	ܐܒܺܝܠܶܐ
I will bless	ܐܶܒܰܪܶܟ
March	ܐܳܕܳܪ
Wages, Payment	ܐܰܓܪܳܐ
Oh!	ܐܘܳܗ
I will make great, I Lift	ܐܰܘܪܶܒ
Way	ܐܘܪܚܳܐ ܐܘܪܚܐ
Hosanna	ܐܘܫܰܥܢܳܐ
I will show you	ܐܚܰܘܶܝܟ
Who, Which, (FS)	ܐܰܝܕܳܐ
September	ܐܝܠܘܠ
Who, Which (M,F, Pl.)	ܐܰܝܠܶܝܢ
As, Like (adj.)	ܐܰܝܟ
Even as	ܐܰܝܟܰܢܳܐ
Tree	ܐܺܝܠܳܢܳܐ
Day (time)	ܐܝܡܳܡܳܐ

Yes	ܐܝܢ
Who, Which (MS)	ܐܝܢܐ
May	ܐܝܪ
There is, There are	ܐܝܬ
Resentment	ܐܟܬܐ
The one has a grudge	ܐܟܬܢ
But	ܐܠܐ
Mother, Mothers	ܐܡܐ ܐܡܗܬܐ
Amen	ܐܡܝܢ
He says	ܐܡܪ
Lamb	ܐܡܪܐ
Doctor, Physician	ܐܣܝܐ
I will make from you	ܐܥܒܕܟܝ
Also	ܐܦ
Wednesday	ܐܪܒܥܒܫܒܐ
Earth	ܐܪܥܐ
Oven, Furnace	ܐܬܘܢܐ
I will say	ܐܡܪ
I will go	ܐܙܠ

ܒ

Shame	ܒܗܬܬܐ
Blessing	ܒܘܪܟܬܐ
Mankind, Humankind	ܒܢܝܢܫܐ
Flesh, Meat, Physical form	ܒܣܪܐ
Created	ܒܪܐ ܒܪܝܐ
Creator	ܒܪܘܝܐ
Blessed	ܒܪܝܟ
Beginning	ܒܪܫܝܬ
In Truth, Truly	ܒܫܪܪܐ
Virgin, Virgins	ܒܬܘܠܬܐ ܒܬܘܠܬܐ

ܓ

He Chose	ܓܒܐ
A brave or valiant man, Giant	ܓܢܒܪܐ
Bandit	ܓܝܣܐ
Vine	ܓܦܬܐ

ܕ

Desert, Wilderness	ܕܒܪܐ
Gold	ܕܗܒܐ
Pure	ܕܟܝܐ

Pure ones	ܕܟܝܢ
Perhaps, If	ܕܠܡܐ
Dawned, Shone	ܕܢܚ
Arm	ܕܪܥܐ
	ܗ
Give	ܗܒ
This (FS) (Near)	ܗܕܐ
That (MS) (Near)	ܗܘ
That (MS) (Distant)	ܗܘ
He is	ܗܘ ܐܝܬܘܗܝ
Mind	ܗܘܢܐ
That (FS) (Near) (Distant)	ܗܝ
These (M, F Plural) (Near)	ܗܠܝܢ
Now, Then, Thus, So, Therefore, For	ܗܟܝܠ
This (MS) (Near)	ܗܢܐ
Those (MP) (Near)	ܗܢܘܢ
Those (MP) (Distant)	ܗܢܘܢ
Those (FP) (Near)	ܗܢܝܢ
Those (FP) (Distant)	ܗܢܝܢ
Turned, Returned, Converted	ܗܦܟ

93

Now	ܗܳܫܳܐ
	ܘ
	ܘ
Time	ܘܰܚܕܳܐ
Just, Righteous	ܘܙܰܕܺܝܩܳܐ
Justice, Righteousness	ܘܙܰܕܺܝܩܽܘܬܳܐ
Victory	ܘܙܳܟܽܘܬܳܐ
Go, Depart, Leave	ܘܰܠ
	ܚ
Sight, Aspect, Example	ܚܙܳܬܳܐ
Sunday	ܚܰܕܒܫܰܒܳܐ
Debts, Offences	ܚܰܘܒܶܐ
Desert, Wilderness	ܚܽܘܪܒܳܐ
He saw	ܚܙܳܐ
Seer	ܚܰܙܳܝܳܐ
June	ܚܙܺܝܪܳܢ
Sinful (F)	ܚܰܛܳܝܬܳܐ
Life	ܚܰܝܶܐ
Thursday	ܚܰܡܫܒܫܰܒܳܐ

Was destroyed	ܚܪܒ
To destroy	ܚܪܒ
Darkness	ܚܫܘܟܐ

ܛ

Happiness, Good fortune	ܛܘܒܐ
Happy, Blessed	ܛܘܒܢܐ
Mountain	ܛܘܪܐ

ܝ

Land, Dry land	ܝܒܫܐ
Day (24 Hrs.)	ܝܘܡܐ
Today, This day	ܝܘܡܢܐ
Canopy, Pavilion, Veil	ܝܪܝܥܬܐ
Inheritance	ܝܪܬܘܬܐ
Teaching, Learning, Doctrine	ܝܘܠܦܢܐ

ܟ

Righteousness, Justice	ܟܐܢܘܬܐ
December	ܟܢܘܢ ܐ
January	ܟܢܘܢ ܒ

Crowd	ܟܢܫܐ
Hungering (ones)	ܟܦܢܝ̈
Cherubim	ܟܪ̈ܘܒܐ
Herald, Messenger, Preacher	ܟܪܘܙܐ
Vineyard	ܟܪܡܐ

ܠ

He put on, He wore or has worn	ܠܒܫ
Luke	ܠܘܩܐ
With, Toward	ܠܘܬ
Bread	ܠܚܡܐ
There is not / There are none	ܠܝܬ
Night	ܠܠܝܐ
Forever	ܠܥܠܡ
Forever and ever	ܠܥܠܡ ܥܠܡܝܢ

ܡ

Faithful	ܡܗܝܡܢܐ
Destroy, Obliterate	ܡܚܩ
Death	ܡܘܬܐ

On account of, Because, For	ܡܛܠ
Meek, Lowly (ones)	ܡܟܝܟ̈ܐ
Humility, Meekness	ܡܟܝܟܘܬܐ
Reproof, Rebuke, Reprimand	ܡܟܣܢܘܬܐ
Preaching, Declaring	ܡܟܪܙܘ
Messenger, Angel	ܡܠܐܟܐ
He spoke	ܡܠܠ
Word	ܡܠܬܐ
Anyone	ܡܢ
Part, Portion	ܡܢܬܐ
Poor ones	ܡܣܟܢ̈ܐ
Baptist, Baptizer	ܡܥܡܕܢܐ
Highest, High region	ܡܪܘܡܐ
Merciful, Compassionate (ones)	ܡܪܚܡܢ̈ܐ
Lady (title), Mistress	ܡܪܬܐ
My lady	ܡܪܬܝ
Praiseworthy, Glorious	ܡܫܒܚܐ
	ܢ
They shall inherit	ܢܐܪܬܘܢ

Prophet	ܢܒܝܐ
Let there be	ܢܗܘܐ
Let be	ܢܗܘܐ
They shall see	ܢܚܙܘܢ
Protector	ܢܛܘܪܐ
Fell, Will fall	ܢܦܠ ܢܦܠ
They shall be satisfied	ܢܣܒܥܘܢ
Temptation	ܢܣܝܘܢܐ
They shall be consoled	ܢܬܒܝܐܘܢ
Let be holy	ܢܬܩܕܫ

ܣ

Put, Place He is putting	ܣܡ ܣܐܡ ܣܐܡ
Silver, Money	ܣܐܡܐ
Hope, Assurance	ܣܒܪܐ
Our needs	ܣܘܢܩܢܝܢ
Fool	ܣܟܠܐ
He ascended, Went up, Climbed	ܣܠܩ
Enemy, One who hates	ܣܢܐܐ

98

	ܥ
Party, Feast, Festival	ܥܐܕܐ
Enter	ܥܒܪ
Made, Will make	ܥܒܕ ܢܥܒܕ
Peacemakers	ܥܒܕܝ ܫܠܡܐ
Maker	ܥܒܘܕܐ
Strength, Force, Might	ܥܘܫܢܐ
Vigilant, Angel	ܥܝܪܐ
People, Nation, Uncle	ܥܡܐ
Labor	ܥܡܠܐ
Peoples, Nations	ܥܡܡܐ
It was or became obscure	ܥܛܐ
Friday	ܥܪܘܒܬܐ
Fled, Ran away	ܥܪܩ
Strong, Mighty	ܥܫܝܢܐ
Prevailed, Became strong	ܥܫܢ

	ܦ
Fruit	ܦܐܪܐ
Met	ܦܓܥ

Salvation	ܦܘܪܩܢܐ
Philip	ܦܝܠܝܦܘܣ
Became insipid, tasteless	ܦܟܗ
Divided	ܦܠܓ
Husbandman, Laborer, Vinedresser	ܦܠܚܐ
Deliver us	ܦܢܢ
Paradise, Park, Garden (Persian)	ܦܪܕܝܣܐ
Prudent, Smart, Booksmart	ܦܪܘܫܐ
Iron	ܦܪܙܠܐ
Flew	ܦܪܚ
Pharoah	ܦܪܥܘܢ
Saved, Will save	ܦܪܩ ܢܦܪܘܩ
Opening	ܦܬܚܝܢ

ܨ

Saint, Saints	ܩܕܝܫܐ ܩܕܝܫܐ
Killed, Will kill	ܩܛܠ ܢܩܛܘܠ
He cried out, He called out	ܩܥܐ
He called, named	ܩܪܐ
Approached	ܩܪܒ

ܪ

Holy Spirit	ܪܘܚܐ ܕܩܘܕܫܐ
Mercy (Pl.)	ܪ̈ܚܡܐ
Rode	ܪܟܒ
Pastor, Shepherd, Bishop	ܪܥܝܐ

ܫ

Forgive	ܫܒܘܩ
Praised, Will Praise	ܫܒܚ ܢܫܒܚ
Left, Departed, Forgave, Permitted, Kept	ܫܒܩ
Saturday	ܫܒܬܐ
Vigilance	ܫܗܪܐ
Boast	ܫܘܒܗܪܐ
Praise, Glory	ܫܘܒܚܐ
Pardon, Forgiveness	ܫܘܒܩܢܐ
Rule over	ܫܠܝܛ
Heaven	ܫܡܝܐ
Simon	ܫܡܥܘܢ
Was pleased	ܫܦܪ
Received (Took)	ܫܩܠ
Tribe, Race, Generation	ܫܪܒܬܐ

True	ܥܕܒܝܕܐ
Truly	ܥܕܒܝܕܐܝܬ
Truth	ܥܕܕܐ
	ܗ
Come	ܬܐ
Let Come	ܬܐܬܐ
Trust, Confidence	ܗܘܓܠܢܐ
Repentance	ܗܢܬܘܗܐ
Tuesday	ܗܠܬܫܒܐ
July	ܬܡܘܙ
There (Adv. of place)	ܬܡܢ
Enter (us)	ܗܥܘܠ
Monday	ܗܕܒܫܒܐ
Honest, Upright, Straight	ܗܪܝܨܐ
Door	ܬܪܥܐ
October	ܬܫܪܝ ܐ
November	ܬܫܪܝ ܒ

Dictionary

English to Aramaic

A

Also	ܐܦ
Amen	ܐܡܝܢ
Angel, Messenger	ܡܠܐܟܐ
Anyone	ܐܢܫ
Approached	ܩܪܒ
April	ܢܝܣܢ
Arm	ܕܪܥܐ
As, like	ܐܝܟ
Ascended, Went up, Climbed (he)	ܣܠܩ
August	ܐܒ

B

Bandit	ܠܣܛܐ
Baptist, Baptizer	ܡܥܡܕܢܐ
Became insipid, tasteless	ܦܟܗ
Beginning, Origin, First Beginning	ܒܪܫܝܬ
Bless you (I will)	ܒܪܟܬܟ

Blessed	ܒܪܝܟ
Blessing	ܒܘܪܟܬܐ
Boast	ܫܘܒܗܪܐ
Brave or valiant man, Giant	ܓܢܒܪܐ
Bread	ܠܚܡܐ
But	ܐܠܐ

C

Called, named (he)	ܩܪܐ
Came (he)	ܐܬܐ
Canopy, Pavilion, Veil	ܩܘܒܬܐ
Cherubim	ܟܪܘܒܐ
Chose (he)	ܓܒܐ
Come	ܬܐ
Consoled (they shall be)	ܢܬܒܝܐܘܢ
Created	ܒܪܐ ܒܪܝ
Creator	ܒܪܘܝܐ
Cried out, called out (he)	ܩܥܐ
Cross	ܨܠܝܒܐ
Crowd	ܟܢܫܐ

D

Darkness	ܚܫܘܟܐ
Dawned, Shone	ܕܢܚ
Day (24hrs.)	ܝܘܡܐ
Day (time)	ܐܝܡܡܐ
Death	ܡܘܬܐ
Debts, Offenses	ܚܘܒܐ
December	ܟܢܘܢ ܐ
Deliver us	ܦܨܢ
Desert, Wilderness	ܡܕܒܪܐ
Desert	ܚܪܒܐ
Destroyed (Devastated)	ܚܪܒ
Destroys, Obliterate	ܡܘܒܕ
Divided	ܦܠܓ
Doctor, Physician	ܐܣܝܐ
Door (Gate)	ܬܪܥܐ

E

Earth	ܐܪܥܐ
Enemy, One who hates	ܣܢܐܐ
Enter	ܥܘܠ

Enter (us)	ܥܘܠܲܢ
Even as	ܐܲܝܟܲܢܵܐ

F

Faithful	ܡܗܲܝܡܢܵܐ
February	ܫܒܵܛ
Fell, will fall	ܢܦܲܠ ܢܸܦܸܠ
Fled, Ran away	ܥܪܲܩ
Flesh, Meat, Physical form	ܒܸܣܪܵܐ
Flew	ܦܪܲܚ
Fool	ܣܲܟ݂ܠܵܐ
Forever	ܠܥܵܠܲܡ
Forever and ever	ܠܥܵܠܲܡ ܥܵܠܡܝܼܢ
Forgive	ܫܒ݂ܘܿܩ
Friday	ܥܪܘܼܒ݂ܬܵܐ
Fruit	ܦܹܐܪܵܐ

G

Give	ܗܲܒ݂
Go, Depart, Leave	ܙܸܠ
Gold	ܕܲܗܒ݂ܵܐ

H

Happiness, Good Fortune	ܛܘܒܐ
Happy, Blessed	ܛܘܒܢܐ
Heaven	ܫܡܝܐ
Herald, Messenger, Preacher	ܟܪܘܙܐ
Highest, High Region	ܡܪܘܡܐ
Holy Spirit	ܪܘܚܐ ܕܩܘܕܫܐ
Honest, Upright, Straight	ܗܓܝܢܐ
Hope, Assurance	ܣܒܪܐ
Hosanna	ܐܘܫܥܢܐ
Humility	ܡܟܝܟܘܬܐ
Hungering (ones)	ܟܦܢܝܢ
Husbandman, Laborer, Vinedresser	ܦܠܚܐ

I

Inherit (they shall)	ܢܐܪܬܘܢ
Inheritance	ܝܪܬܘܬܐ
Insipid	ܦܟܗ
Iron	ܦܪܙܠܐ
Is	ܗܘ ܐܝܬܘܗܝ

107

J

January	ܟܢܘܢ:ܒ
Judah	ܝܗܘܕܐ
Judea	ܝܗܘܕ
July	ܛܡܘܙ
June	ܚܙܝܪܢ
Just, Righteous	ܘܕܝܩܐ
Justice	ܟܐܢܘܬܐ

K

Killed, Will kill	ܩܛܠ ܢܩܛܘܠ

L

Lady (title), Mistress	ܡܪܬܐ
Lady (my)	ܡܪܬܝ
Lamb	ܐܡܪܐ
Land, Dry land	ܝܒܫܐ
Left, Departed, Forgave, Permitted, Kept	ܫܒܩ
Let be	ܢܗܘܐ
Let be holy	ܢܬܩܕܫ
Let there be	ܢܗܘܐ

Life	ܚܲܝܹ̈ܐ

M

Made, will make	ܥܒܸܕ ܒܸܥܒܸܕ
Maker	ܥܵܒ݂ܘܿܕܵܐ
Mankind, Humankind	ܐ̄ܢܵܫܘܼܬܵܐ
Make you (I will)	ܒܸܥܒܸܕܘܼܟ݂
Make great (I will)	ܒܘܼܪܸܒ݂
March	ܐܵܕܲܪ
May	ܐܝܼܵܪ
Meek, Lowly (ones)	ܡܲܟ݁ܝܼܟܹ̈ܐ
Merciful, Compassionate (ones)	ܡܪܲܚܡܵܢܹ̈ܐ
Mercy (pl., singular)	ܪܲܚܡܹ̈ܐ
Met	ܦܓܲܥ
Mind	ܗܵܘܢܵܐ
Monday	ܬܪܹܝܢܒܫܲܒܵܐ
Mother, Mothers	ܐܸܡܵܐ ܐܸܡܵܗܵ̈ܬܹܐ
Mountain	ܛܘܼܪܵܐ
Mourners	ܐܲܒ݂ܝܼܠܹ̈ܐ

N

Needs (our)	ܚܫܚ̈ܬܢ
Night	ܠܠܝܐ
November	ܬܫܪܝܢ: ܒ
Now, Then, Thus, So, Therefore, For	ܗܟܝܠ
Now	ܗܫܐ

O

Obscure (It was or became)	ܥܡܛ
October	ܬܫܪܝܢ: ܐ
Oh!	ܐܘ ܐܘ
Opening (They are open)	ܦܬܝܚܝܢ
Oven, Furnace	ܬܢܘܪܐ

P

Paradise, Park, Garden (Persian)	ܦܪܕܝܣܐ
Pardon, Forgiveness	ܥܘܓܢܐ
Part, Portion	ܡܢܬܐ
Party, Feast, Festival	ܚܓܐ
Pastor, Shepherd, Bishop	ܪܥܝܐ
Peacemakers	ܥܒ̈ܕܝ ܫܠܡܐ
People, Nation, pl.	ܥܡ̈ܡܬ ܥܡܐ

110

Perhaps	ܕܠܡܐ
Pharaoh	ܦܪܥܘܢ
Philip	ܦܝܠܝܦܘܣ
Was pleased	ܨܒܐ
Praise, Glory	ܫܘܒܚܐ
Praised, Will praise	ܫܒܚ ܢܫܒܚ
Praiseworthy, Glorious	ܡܫܒܚܐ
Preaching, Declaring	ܡܟܪܙܘ
Prevailed, Became strong	ܥܫܢ
Prophet	ܢܒܝܐ
Protector	ܢܛܘܪܐ
Prudent, Smart	ܦܪܘܫܐ
Pure	ܕܟܝܐ
Pure ones	ܕܟܝܐ
Put, Place	ܣܡ ܣܘܡ ܣܐܡ
Put on (he), he wore or has worn	ܠܒܫ

Q

R

| Received (took) | ܩܒܠ |
| Repentance | ܬܝܒܘܬܐ |

Reproof, Rebuke. Reprimand	ܡܟܣܢܘܬܐ
Resentment (One who carries grudge)	ܢܛܪܢܐ
Resurrection, Recovery, Revival	ܩܘܝܡܐ
Rode	ܪܟܒ
Rule over	ܫܠܛ

S

Saint, Saints	ܩܕܝܫܐ ܩܕܝܫܐ̈
Salvation	ܦܘܪܩܢܐ
Sat down	ܝܬܒ
Satisfied, They shall be	ܢܣܒܥܘܢ
Saturday	ܫܒܬܐ
Saved, Will save	ܦܪܩ ܢܦܪܘܩ
Saw	ܚܙܐ
Says (he), is saying	ܐܡܪ
See (they shall)	ܢܚܙܘܢ
Seer	ܚܙܝܐ
September	ܐܝܠܘܠ
Shame	ܒܗܬܬܐ
Show you (I will)	ܐܚܘܝܟ
Sight, Aspect, Example	ܚܙܬܐ

Silver, Money	ܣܐܡܐ
Simon	ܫܡܥܘܢ
Sinful (f)	ܚܛܝܬܐ
Spoke (he)	ܡܠܠ
Strength, Force, Might	ܚܝܠܐ
Strong, Mighty	ܚܣܝܢܐ
Sunday	ܚܕܒܫܒܐ

T

Teaching, Learning, Doctrine	ܝܘܠܦܢܐ
Temptation	ܢܣܝܘܢܐ
That (MS Near)	ܗܘ
That (FS Near)	ܗܝ
That (MS Distannt)	ܗܘ
That (FS Distant)	ܗܝ
There (adv. of place)	ܬܡܢ
There is / are	ܐܝܬ
There is not / are none	ܠܝܬ
These (M,F Plural)	ܗܠܝܢ
Thirsting (ones)	ܨܗܝܐ
This (MS Near)	ܗܢܐ

This (FS Near)	ܗܳܕܶܐ
Those (MP Near)	ܗܳܢܽܘܢ
Those (FP, Near)	ܗܳܠܶܝܢ
Those (MP Distant)	ܗܳܢܽܘܢ
Those (FP, Distant)	ܗܳܢܶܝܢ
Thursday	ܚܰܡܫܽܘܫܰܒܳܐ
Time	ܙܰܒܢܳܐ
Today, This day	ܝܰܘܡܳܢܳܐ
Tree	ܐܺܝܠܳܢܳܐ
Tribe, Race, Generation	ܫܰܪܒܬܳܐ
True	ܫܰܪܺܝܪܳܐ
Truly	ܫܰܪܺܝܪܳܐܝܺܬ
In truth, Truly	ܒܫܪܳܪܳܐ
Trust, Confidence	ܬܽܘܟܠܳܢܳܐ
Truth	ܫܪܳܪܳܐ
Tuesday	ܬܠܳܬܒܫܰܒܳܐ
Turned, Returned, Converted	ܗܦܰܟ
U	
V	
Vigilance	ܙܗܺܝܪܽܘܬܳܐ
Vigilant	ܙܗܺܝܪܳܐ

Vine	ܒܩܢܐ
Vineyard	ܟܪܡܐ
Virgin, Virgins	ܒܬܘܠܬܐ ܒܬܘܠܬܐ

W

Wages, Payment	ܐܓܪܐ
Way (Pl.)	ܐܘܪܚܐ ܐܘܪܚܬܐ
Which, Who (MS)	ܐܝܢܐ
Which, Who (FS)	ܐܝܕܐ
Which Who (M, F Plural)	ܐܝܠܝܢ
Will, Wish, Desire	ܨܒܝܢܐ
With, Toward	ܠܘܬ
Witness	ܣܗܕܘܬܐ
Word	ܡܠܬܐ

X

Y

Yes	ܐܝܢ

Z

ABOUT THE AUTHOR
Michael J. Bazzi

The Rev. Fr. Michael J. Bazzi, L.S.T., (Emeritus) pastored St. Peter Chaldean Catholic Church in El Cajon, San Diego, since 1987. Fr. Michael also served as a professor of modern and classical Aramaic at Cuyamaca College in El Cajon from 1989-2020. Fr. Michael is a distinguished Bible authority, author, teacher, linguist, translator, and pastoral counselor.

Born in Tilkepe, Iraq, a suburb of Nineveh, he graduated seminary at St. Peter's College, Baghdad, and was ordained into the priesthood in that same year, 1964. He served eight years in Tilkepe as an assisting priest speaking his native language of Aramaic, as well as Arabic. He then travelled to the Vatican in Rome where he earned a Masters Degree in Pastoral Theology. While in Italy he gained a broad knowledge of the Italian and French languages.

Fr. Michael arrived in Oshkosh — Green Bay, Wisconsin in 1974. Here he taught and preached Scripture from the Aramaic point of view. Later, he established parishes in Oak Park and Troy, Michigan, and in 1983-85, served in Los Angeles, CA. Fr. Michael moved to San Diego in 1985.

Fr. Michael was the San Diego Law Enforcement Association's Citizen of the Year in 2010.

Books by Fr. Michael J. Bazzi:

Tilkepe
The Life of Tilkepnaye
Chaldean Nation
Classical Aramaic 1 & II
Modern Aramaic Vol. I & II
Beginners Handbook of the Aramaic Language
Read and Write Aramaic (for children)
Know Your Faith
Who are the Chaldeans?
Chaldeans Past and Present
The Book of Matthew
The Pentatuch

ABOUT THE AUTHOR
Rocco A. Errico

Dr. Rocco A. Errico is an ordained minister, international lecturer and author, spiritual counselor, and one of the nation's leading Bible scholars working from the original Aramaic *Peshitta* texts. For ten years, he studied intensively with Dr. George M. Lamsa, Th. D., (1890-1975), world-renowned Assyrian biblical scholar and translator of the Holy Bible from the Ancient Eastern Text. Dr. Errico is proficient in Aramaic and Hebrew exegesis, helping thousands of readers and seminar participants understand how the Semitic context of culture, language, idioms, symbolism, mystical style, psychology, and literary amplification—the Seven Keys that unlock the Bible—are essential to understanding the ancient spiritual document.

Dr. Errico is the recipient of numerous awards and academic degrees, including a Doctorate in Philosophy from the School of Christianity in Los Angeles; a Doctorate in Divinity from St. Ephrem's Institute in Sweden; and a Doctorate in Sacred Theology from the School of Christianity in Los Angeles. In 1993, the American Apostolic University College of Seminarians awarded him a Doctorate of Letters. He also holds a special title of Teacher, Prime Exegete, *Maplana d'miltha dalaha*, among the Federation of St. Thomas Christians of the order of Antioch. In 2002, Dr. Errico was inducted into the Morehouse College Collegium of Scholars.

Dr. Errico is a featured speaker at conferences, symposia, and seminars throughout the United States, Canada, Mexico, and Europe and has been a regular contributor for over 35 years to Science of Mind Magazine, a monthly journal founded in 1927. He began his practice as an ordained minister and pastoral counselor in the mid-1950's and during the next three decades served in churches and missions in Missouri, Texas, Mexico, and California. Throughout his public work, Dr. Errico has stressed the nonsectarian, open interpretation of Biblical spirituality, prying it free from 2000 years of rigid orthodoxy, which, according to his research, is founded on incorrect translations of the Aramaic texts.

In 1970, Dr. Errico established the Noohra Foundation in San Antonio, Texas, as a non-profit, non-sectarian spiritual educational organization devoted to helping people of all faiths to understand the Near Eastern background and Aramaic interpretations of the Bible. In 1976, Dr. Errico relocated the Noohra Foundation in Irvine, California, where it flourished for the next 17 years. For seven years, the Noohra Foundation operated in Santa Fe, New Mexico, and in September 2001, it relocated to Smyrna, Georgia, where Dr. Errico served as Dean of Biblical Studies for Dr. Barbara King's School of Ministry — Hillside Chapel and Truth Center in Atlanta.

Under the auspices of the Noohra Foundation, Dr. Errico continues to lecture for colleges, civic groups and churches of various denominations in the United States, Canada, Mexico and Europe.

Books By Dr. Errico

Let There Be Light: The Seven Keys
And There Was Light
Setting A Trap For God: The Aramaic Prayer of Jesus
The Mysteries of Creation: The Genesis Story
The Message of Matthew: Am Annotated Parallel Aramaic-English Gospel of Matthew
La Antigua Oracion Aramea De Jesus: El Padrenuestro
Das Aramaische Vaterunser
Es Werde Licht
Otto Accordi Con Dio: il Padre Nostro orginario

Commentaries By Dr. Rocco A. Errico and Dr. George M Lamsa:

Aramaic Light on the Gospel of Matthew, Aramaic Light on the Gospels of Mark and Luke, Aramaic Light on the Gospel of John, Aramaic Light on the Acts of the Apostles, Aramaic Light on Romans thorugh 2 Corinthians, Aramaic Light on Galatians through Hebrews, Aramaic Light on James through Revelation, Aramaic Light on Genesis, Aramaic Light on Exodus through Deuteronomy, Aramaic Light on Joshua through 2 Chronicles, Aramaic Light on Ezra through the Song of Solomon, and Aramaic Light on Isaiah, Jerimiah, and Lamentations, Aramaic Light on Ezekiel, Daniel, and the Minor Prophets.

To order these and other books, or if you are interested in contacting Dr. Errico about a personal appearance, please contact:

Noohra Foundation
PMB 343
4480 South Cobb Dr. SE Ste. H
Smyrna, GA 30080

www.noohra.com
Phone: 678-260-5021

Titles by Let in the Light Publishing:

Aramaic Language Chaldean Dialect

Beginner's Handbook of the Aramaic Chaldean Alphabets

Advanced Handbook of Modern Aramaic Language ChaldeanVol. II

Chaldean Nation (English / Arabic)

Chaldeans Past and Present

Classical Aramaic I

Classical Aramaic II

A High School Tennis Coach's Handbook: For Parents, Players, & Coaches

The Life of Tilkepnaye (Paperback Trilingual / Hardback English)

Preserving the Chaldean Aramaic Language

Read and Write the Modern Aramaic in Chaldean Dialogue

For more information, or to purchase, please visit our website:
www.letinthelightpublishing.com

www.ingramcontent.com/pod-product-compliance
Lightning Source LLC
Chambersburg PA
CBHW061811230426

43665CB00033BA/3000